The Ages of Man

by Thornton Wilder

A SAMUEL FRENCH ACTING EDITION

SAMUEL FRENCH

FOUNDED 1830

SAMUELFRENCH.COM

MUSIC USE NOTE

**IMPORTANT BILLING AND CREDIT
REQUIREMENTS**

FOREWORD TO *THE SINS* AND *AGES*

Welcome to a new collection of Thornton Wilder's last plays—a series of one acts that were part of his extravagantly ambitious project to create two seven-play cycles based on the deadly sins and the ages of man. From the time he began dreaming up plays as a boy, Wilder's vision of the theater transcended conventional boundaries, and up to the end of his life his vision continually evolved and expanded, as these plays demonstrate.

In 1956, Wilder began working on what would prove to be his final dramatic works, seeking not only to explore the theatrical possibilities inherent in the sins and ages, but (as he phrased it in his private journal on Christmas Day, 1960) to "offer each play in the series as representing, also, a different mode of playwriting: Grand Guignol, Chekhov, Noh play, etc., etc." In short, he envisioned nothing less than a *tour de force* of dramatic theme and form encapsulated in the economy and intensity of the one act play.

Wilder did not complete the challenge he set for himself, but he came close. The surviving work enriches his dramatic legacy and deserves to be remembered as more than a footnote to his lifelong conviction (written soon after *Our Town* opened on Broadway in 1938): "The theater offers to imaginative narration its highest possibilities."

The *Sins* and *Ages* Then and Now

A brief overview of the history of these plays will help readers "place" them in Wilder's career as a dramatist. Two *Sins* (*Pride* and *Sloth*) premiered in English at a special event in Berlin in 1957 (with Wilder performing in *Pride*). For reasons that have never been clear, for he enjoyed the experience and felt that plays did well, he withdrew them from the event. That same year a third *Sin* (*Gluttony*), written as the satyr play for Wilder's full length drama, *The Alcestiad*, proved successful in its premiere on the stage of Zurich's fabled Schauspielhaus.

Five years passed before the continuation of his ambitious scheme appeared on a stage in the United States. In January 1962, two new *Ages* (*Infancy* and *Childhood*) and a new *Sin* (*Lust*) opened at Circle in the Square, then located Off Broadway on Bleecker Street, to the reported largest pre-opening advanced sale in that stage's then 11-year history. Billed as "Plays for Bleecker Street," the show ran for 349 performances.

Then silence. After "Plays for Bleecker Street" closed, no more *Sins* or *Ages* appeared. When Thornton Wilder died in 1975 the public record of his ambitious fourteen plays scheme contained only four plays—two *Ages* (*Infancy* and *Childhood*) and two *Sins* (*Lust* and *Gluttony*).

Today, as evidenced by the content of this volume, eleven of Wilder's *Sins* and *Ages* are available for production: a completed cycle of the seven deadly sins and four of the seven ages of man.[1] The source of the seven "new" plays is no secret. The missing pieces were found in Thornton Wilder's archives at Yale. From this source, starting in 1995, his literary executor and family released the two plays withdrawn in 1957, a completed *Avarice*, and four additional titles (*Youth, The Rivers Under the Earth* [*Middle Age*][2], *Envy* and *Wrath*) recovered by the actor, director and close friend of Wilder's, F.J. O'Neil. (Mr. O'Neil's valuable notes on the origin of each of these missing links follow the text of each play.)

The public reception of Thornton Wilder's long lost and new plays was gratifying. *Sloth* was selected as one of the Best American Short Plays of 1994-95. In 1997, the Centenary of the playwright's birth, Kevin Kline starred in a premiere reading in New York of *Avarice*, and the works recovered by Mr. O'Neil served as the center pieces of Actors Theatre of Louisville's 13th Annual Brown-Forman Classics in Context Festival. Finally, as the capstone to the Centenary celebration, TCG Press in 1997 published the eleven *Sins* and *Ages* in Volume I of *The Collected Short Plays of Thornton Wilder*.

Wilder never followed conventional theatrical practice. As a young writer in his *Classic One Act Plays* of 1931, he swept away scenery and played provocative games with time and place. In these *Sins* and *Ages*, his farewell as a playwright, he is no less adventurous by way of settings, techniques, stage-craft and themes. One artistic trend of the day especially "fired his imagination" where these plays are concerned: his passionate belief in the value of the arena stage. "The boxed set play," he wrote in 1961, "encourages the anecdote...The unencumbered stage encourages the truth in everyone." Wilder felt so strongly that audiences should be seated as close to the actors as possible that Samuel French, for several years, was only permitted to license these plays to companies agreeing to perform them on a three-sided thrust or arena stage.

* * *

As part of its celebration of Wilder's one act plays, Samuel French and the Wilder family take great pleasure in issuing new acting editions for the *Sins* and *Ages* that were long in print and, for the first time, acting editions for the seven "new" Wilder works. We invite those performing or teaching these plays to visit www.thorntonwilder.com for additional information.

Tappan Wilder
Literary Executor for Thornton Wilder

---

1 No additional one acts remain to be discovered in Thornton Wilder's archives at Yale.
2 We believe that Wilder intended *Rivers Under the Earth* to represent middle age.

CONTENTS

INFANCY

A Comedy

CHARACTERS

OFFICER AVONZINO
MISS MILLIE WILCHICK, a nursemaid
TOMMY, a baby in her care
MRS. BOKER
MOE, her baby boy

SETTING

Central Park in New York City. The 1920s.

(One or more large park benches. Some low stools at the edges of the stage indicate bushes.)

(Enter **OFFICER AVONZINO**, *a policeman from the Keystone comic movies with a waterfall mustache, thick black eyebrows and a large silver star. Swinging his billy club jauntily, he shades his eyes and peers down the paths for trouble. Reassured, he extracts a small memorandum book from an inner pocket of his jacket and reads:)*

AVONZINO. "Wednesday, April 26..." Right. "Centra' Park, Patrol Section Eleven, West, Middle." Right! "Lieutenant T. T. Avonzino." Correct. Like Tomaso Tancredo Avonzino. "Eight to twelve; two to six. Special Orders: Suspect – mad dog, black with white spots. Suspect – old gentleman, silk hat, pinches nurses." *(reflects)* Pinch babies okay; pinch nurses, nuisance. *(puts the book away, strolls, then takes it out again for further instructions)* Probable weather: late morning, precipitation – precipitation like rain. *(strolls)* Seven to eight-thirty, no nuisances. Millionaires on horses; horses on millionaires. Young gents running in underwear; old gents running in underwear. *(reflects)* Running in underwear, okay; *walking* in underwear, nuisance. Eight-thirty to nine-thirty, everybody late for working, rush-rush, no time for nuisances. Nine-thirty to twelve, babies. One thousand babies with ladies. Nuisances plenty: old gents poisoning pigeons; ladies stealing baby carriages. Nuisances in bushes: young gents and young girls taking liberties. *(hotly)* Why can't they do their nuisances at home? That's what homes are for: to do your nuisances in. *(He shields his eyes and peers toward the actors' entrance at the back of the stage; emotionally.)* Here she comes! Miss'a Wilchick! *Baby!* – prize baby of Centra' Park.

AVONZINO. *(cont.) (He extracts a handbook from another pocket of his jacket.)* "Policeman's Guide. Lesson Six: Heart Attacks and Convulsions." No. No. "Lesson Sixteen: Frostbite." No! "Lesson Eleven:..." Ha! "An officer exchanges no personal remarks wid de public." Crazy! *(in dreamy ecstasy)* Oh, personal re-marks. It's personal remarks dat make-a de world go round; dat make-a de birds sing. *(indignantly)* Nobody, *nobody* wid flesh and blood can live widout'a personal re-marks. Ha! She comes!... *(He steals off by the aisle through the audience.)*

(Enter from the back **MISS MILLIE WILCHICK,** *pushing Tommy's baby carriage.* **TOMMY,** *now invisible in the carriage, is to be played by a full-grown man.* **MILLIE** *brings the carriage to rest by a bench. She peers up the various paths in search of* **OFFICER AVONZINO.** *Disappointed, she prepares to make herself comfortable. From the foot of the carriage she brings out a box of chocolates, another of marshmallows, and a novel. Before sitting down she talks into the carriage.)*

MILLIE. ...lil sweet lovums. Miss Millie's lil lover, aren't you? Yes, you are. I could squeeze lil Tommy to death, yes. I could. Kiss-kiss-kiss, yes, I could. *(again peering down the paths)* Don't know where Mr. Policeman is! Big handsome Officer Avonzino. He take care of Miss Millie and lil lover-boy Tommy...Hmm...Maybe he come by and by. *(She sits on the bench and selects a candy.)* ... Peppermint...strawb'ry?...Well, and a marshmallow. *(She opens the novel at the first page and reads with great deliberation.)* "Doris was not strictly beautiful, but when she passed, men's heads turned to gaze at her with pleasure. Doris was not strictly beautiful, but..." *(a squeal of joy)* Oh, they *don't* write like that any more!! Oh, I'm going to enjoy this book. Let's see how it ends. First, there must be one of those chawclut cream centers. *(She turns to the last page of the novel.)* "He drew her to him, pressing his lips on hers. 'Forever,' he said. Doris closed her eyes. 'Forever,' she said. The end."

(delighted cry) They don't write like that any more. "For e...e...ever." Could I say "forever," if his lips... "e-e-v"...were pressed on mine? *(She closes her eyes and experiments.)* ...e...ver...for...e...Yes, I guess it could be done. *(She starts dreaming.)* Oh, I *know* I could write a novel. *(She dreams.)*

(Slowly TOMMY's hands can be seen gripping the side of his carriage. With great effort he pulls himself up until his head appears. He is wearing a lace-trimmed cap.)

TOMMY. Fur...evvah...Do-rus...nah...strigly bootoody... *(fretfully)* I can't say it...boody-fill...Why don't they teach me to say it? I want to LEARN and they won't teach me. Do-rua nah stackly...boody...Fur evvah... *(near to wailing)* Time's going by. I'm getting owe-uld. And nobody is showing me *anything*. I wanta make a house. I wanta make a house. I wanta make a bay-beee. Nobody show-ow-ow-s me how-ta.

MILLIE. *(waking up)* Tommy! What are you crying about? Has 'a got a little stummyache? Has 'a got a foot caught? No. *(leaning over him, suddenly severe)* Has Tommy wet his bed?!! No. No. Then's what's a matter?

TOMMY. Wanta make a house!

MILLIE. Wants to be petted, yes.

TOMMY. *(violently)* Wanta make a baybeee!

MILLIE. Miss Millie's lil lover wants a little attention.

TOMMY. *(fortissimo)* Chawclut. Chawclut. Wanta eat what you're eating. Wanta eat what you smell of...chawclut.

MILLIE. Now don't you climb up. You'll fall out. It's terrible the way you're growing.

TOMMY. Put me on the ground. I wanta learn to walk. I wanta walk. I wanta walk. I wanta find things to *eat.*

MILLIE. *(sternly)* Now Miss Millie's going to spank you. Crying for nothing. You ought to be ashamed of yourself.

(She stands joggling the baby carriage with one hand and holding the opened novel with the other.)

MILLIE. *(cont.)* "This little pig went to *mar-ket*." There! "This little pig…" shhshh – shh! "Doris was not strictly beautiful, but…" Oh, I read that. "This little pig stayed at home." *(She looks into the carriage with great relief.)* God be praised in His glory, babies get tired soon…Asleep. *(She walks across the stage; then suddenly stops.)* I don't know what I'm going to do. My life is hell. Here I am, a good-looking girl almost thirty and *nothing ever happens.* Everybody's living, except me. Everybody's happy, except ME!! *(She returns, sobbing blindly to the baby carriage.)* Those silly novels – I hate them – just gab-gab-gab. Now I'm crying so I can't see which is pineapple. *(She chances to look in the direction of the aisle through the audience.)* Oh, my God, there comes Officer Avonzino. *(She clasps her hands in fervent prayer.)* Oh, my God, help a girl! If you ever helped a girl, help her now!

*(She rapidly hides novel and candy under **TOMMY**'s blankets, and takes out another book. She arranges herself at one end of the bench and pretends to fall into a reverie.)*

*(Enter **OFFICER AVONZINO** through the audience. He steals behind **MILLIE** and puts his hands over her eyes. The following passage is very rapid.)*

AVONZINO. You've got one guessing coming to you! *Who* is in Centra' Park? Maybe who?

MILLIE. Oh, I don't know. I really don't.

AVONZINO. You've got two guessings. Maybe the mayor of Newa-York, maybe him, you think? Now you got one guessing. Maybe T. T. Avonzino – like somebody you know, somebody you seen before.

MILLIE. Oh! Officer Avonzino!!

(He leaps on the bench beside her. She is kept busy removing his hands from her knees.)

AVONZINO. Somebody you know. Somebody you seen before.

MILLIE. Officer, you must behave. You really must behave.

AVONZINO. Action! I believe is a action! Personal remarks and da action.

(**TOMMY** *has raised himself and is staring enormous-eyed and with great disapproval at these goings-on.*)

TOMMY. *(loudly)* Ya! Ya! Ya! Ya! Ya!

(**OFFICER AVONZINO** *is thunderstruck. He jumps up as though caught out of order by his superior. He stands behind the bench adjusting his tie and coat and star.*)

MILLIE. Why, what's the matter, Mr. Avonzino?

AVONZINO. *(low and terse)* Him. Looka at him. Looka at him, looking.

TOMMY. Ya. Ya. Ya.

MILLIE. Go to sleep, Tommy. Just nice policerman. Tommy's friend. Go to sleep.

TOMMY. *(one last warning, emphatically)* Ya!

(He disappears.)

MILLIE. But, Officer, he's just a *baby*. He doesn't understand one little thing.

AVONZINO. *(blazing, but under his breath)* Oh no, oh no, oh no, oh no – he got thoughts. Turn-a de carriage around. I no wanta see that face.

MILLIE. *(turning the carriage)* I'm surprised at you. He's just a dear little baby. A dear little…animal.

AVONZINO. Miss Wilchick, I see one thousand babies a day. They got *ideas*.

MILLIE. *(laughing girlishly)* Why, Mr. Avonzino, you're like the author of this book I've been reading. – Dr. Kennick. He says babies are regular geniuses in their first fourteen months. He says: you know why babies sleep all the time? Because they're learning all the time, they get tired by learning. Geniuses, he says, imagine!

AVONZINO. *What* he say?

MILLIE. They learn more than they'll ever learn again. And faster. Like hands and feet; and to focus your eyes. And like walking and talking. He says their brains are exploding with power.

AVONZINO. What he say?

MILLIE. Well – after about a year they stop being geniuses. Dr. Kennick says the reason why we aren't geniuses is that we weren't brought up right: we were stopped.

AVONZINO. That's a right. He gotta the right idea. Miss Wilchick, I see one thousand babies a day. And what I say is: stop 'em. That's your business, Miss Wilchick; that's my business. There's too many ingeniouses in Centra' Park right now: stop 'em.

(**TOMMY** *begins to howl.* **AVONZINO** *points at him with his billy club.*)

What did I tell you? They all understand English. North' a Eighth Street they all understand English.

MILLIE. *(leaning over Tommy's carriage)* There, there. Nice policeman don't mean *one* word of it.

AVONZINO. *(Looking at the actors' entrance; they are both shouting to be heard.)* Here comes another brains. I go now.

MILLIE. Oh, that must be Mrs. Boker – I'm so sorry this happened, Mr. Avonzino.

AVONZINO. I see you later, maybe – when you get permission from the professor – permission in writing, Miss Wilchick. *(He goes out through the audience.)*

(*Enter* **MRS. BOKER** *pushing Moe's carriage.* **MOE** *starts crying in sympathy with* **TOMMY**. *Both women shout.*)

MRS. BOKER. What's the matter with Tommy – good morning – on such a fine day?

MILLIE. *(leaning over* **TOMMY***)* What's a matter?

TOMMY. CHAWCLUT!! STRAWB'RY!! I'm hungree.

MILLIE. Really, I don't know what ails the child.

MRS. BOKER. *(leaning over Moe's carriage; beginning loud but gradually lowering her voice as both babies cease howling)* …K…L…M…N…O…P…Q…R…S…T… Have you ever noticed, Miss Wilchick, that babies get quiet when you say the alphabet to them? …W…X…Y…A…B… C…D… I don't understand it. Moe is mad about the alphabet. Same way with the multiplication table.

MRS. BOKER. *(cont.) (to* **MOE,** *who is now silent)* Three times five are fifteen. Three times six are eighteen. When my husband has to keep Moe quiet: the multiplication table! Never fails! My husband calls him Isaac Newton. – Seven times five are thirty-five. Eight times five are forty. Never fails.

MILLIE. *(intimidated)* Really?

MRS. BOKER. *(pointing to the silent carriages)* Well, look for yourself! Isn't silence grand? *(She sits on a bench and starts taking food out of* **MOE**'s *carriage.)* Now, dear, have some potato chips. Or pretzels. What do you like?

MILLIE. Well, you have some of my marshmallows and candy.

MRS. BOKER. Marshmallows! Oh, I know I shouldn't! – Have you noticed that being around babies makes you think of eating all the time? I don't know why that is. *(pushing* **MILLIE** *in raucous enjoyment of the joke)* Like, being with babies makes us like babies. And you know what *they* think about!!

MILLIE. *(convulsed)* Oh, Mrs. Boker, what will you say next! – How is Moe, Mrs. Boker?

MRS. BOKER. *(her mouth full)* How *is* he!! Sometimes I wish he'd be sick for *one* day – just to give me a present. *(lowering her voice)* I don't have to tell you what life with a baby is: *(looking around circumspectly)* It's *war – one long war.* – Excuse me, I can't talk while he's listening. *(She rises and wheels* **MOE**'s *carriage to a distance; returning, she continues in a lowered voice.)* My husband believes that Moe understands every word we say.

MILLIE. Mrs. Boker!

MRS. BOKER. I don't know what to believe, but one thing I do know: that baby lies on the floor and listens to every word we say. At first my husband took to spelling out words, you know – but Albert Einstein, there – in two weeks he got them all. He would *look* at my husband, *look* at him with those big eyes! And then my husband took to talking in Yiddish – see what I mean? – but no! In two weeks Albert Einstein got Yiddish.

MILLIE. But, Mrs. Boker!! It's just a baby! He don't understand *one word.*

MRS. BOKER. *You* know that. *I* know that. But *(pointing to the carriage)* does *he* know that? It's driving my husband crazy. "Turn it in and get a dog," he says. "I didn't ask for no prodigy," he says. "All I wanted was a baby – " *(lowering her voice)* Of course, most of the time my husband worships Moe…only…only we don't know what to do with him, as you might say.

MILLIE. Oh, you imagine it, Mrs. Boker!

MRS. BOKER. Listen to me! – Have some of these pretzels; they'll be good after those sweets. Listen to me, Junior's at the crawling stage. He does fifty miles a day. My husband calls him Christopher Columbus. – My husband's stepped on him five times.

MILLIE. Mrs. Boker! You've got a playpen, haven't you?

MRS. BOKER. PLAYPEN!! He's broke two, hasn't he? We can't afford to buy no lion's cage, Miss Wilchick – besides, Macy's don't sell them. Now listen to me: Christopher Columbus follows us wherever we go, see? When I get supper – there he is! He could make a gefilte fish tomorrow. That child – mad about the bathroom! Know what I mean? My husband says he has a "something" mind – you know: d. i. r. t. y.

MILLIE. Mrs. Boker.

MRS. BOKER. Sometimes I wish I had a girl – only it'd be just my luck to get one of those Joans of Arcs.
(MOE starts to howl.)
There he goes! Like I said: understands *every* word we say. Now watch this: *(She leans over MOE's carriage, holding a handkerchief before her mouth.)* You mustn't let them smell what you've been eating, *or else* – Listen, Moe, like I was telling you: New York City is divided into five boroughs. There's the Bronx, Moe, and Brooklyn and Queens –
(MOE quiets almost at once.)
See how it works? – Richmond and Manhattan. – It's crazy, I know, but what can I do about that? – Yes, Manhattan; the largest, like I told you, is Manhattan. Yes, Manhattan.

(She looks in the carriage. Silence.) Isn't it a blessing that they get tired so soon? He's exhausted by the boroughs already.

MILLIE. But he doesn't understand a word of it!!

MRS. BOKER. What has understanding got to do with it, Miss Wilchick? I don't understand the telephone, but I *telephone.*

*(***TOMMY*** *has raised his head and is listening big-eyed.)*

TOMMY. N'Yak Citee divi fife burrs. Manha...Manha... Manha... *(He starts crying with frustration.)* I can't *say* it. I can't *say* it.

MRS. BOKER. Now yours is getting excited.

TOMMY. I can't talk and nobody'll teach me. I can't talk...

MRS. BOKER. *(loud)* Go over and put him to sleep.

MILLIE. *(loud)* But I don't know the boroughs. Please, Mrs. Boker, just once, you show me.

MRS. BOKER. I'll try something else. Watch this! Listen, Tommy, are you listening? "I pledge legions to my flag and to the republic in which it stands." You were a girl scout, weren't you? "Something something invisible with liberty and justice for all."

*(***TOMMY*** *has fallen silent.)*

"I pledge legions to my flag..."

MILLIE. *(awed)* Will anything work?

MRS. BOKER. *(lowering her voice)* They don't like those lullabies and "This little pig went to market." See, they like it *serious.* There's nothing in the world so serious like a baby. – Well, now we got a little quiet again.

MILLIE. Mrs. Boker, can I ask you a question about Moe?... Take one of these; it's pineapple inside...Is Moe, like they say, housebroken?

MRS. BOKER. Moe?! Gracious sakes! Moe makes a great show of it. I guess there isn't a thing in the world that interests Moe like going to his potty. *(She laughs.)* When he wants to make us a present: *off* he goes! When he's angry at us…oh, no! He plays it like these violinists play their violin…which reminds me!… *(looking about her speculatively)* Do you suppose…I could just…slip behind these bushes a minute?…is that police officer around?

MILLIE. Well-ah…Officer Avonzino is awfully particular about nuisances, what he calls nuisances. Maybe you could go over to the avenue there – there's a branch library…

MRS. BOKER. Will you be an angel and watch Moe for me? If he starts to cry, give him the days of the week and the months of the year. He *loves* them. – Now where's this library?

MILLIE. Why, the Museum of National History's right over there.

MRS. BOKER. *(scream of pleasure)* Museum of Natural History!! How could I have forgotten that! Just full of animals. Of *course*! I won't be a minute, dear!…

(They exchange good-byes. **MRS. BOKER** *goes out.* **MILLIE** *eyes Moe's carriage apprehensively, then seats herself and resumes her novel at the last page.)*

MILLIE. "Roger came into the room. His fine strong face still bore the marks of the suffering he had experienced." Oh! I imagine his wife died. Isn't that wonderful! He's *free*! "He drew her to him, pressing his lips on hers. 'Forever,' he said." Oh! "For-ever."

(In a moment, she is asleep.)

*(***TOMMY*** *pulls himself up and stares at* **MOE** *'s carriage.)*

TOMMY. Moe!…Moe!

MOE. *(surging up furiously)* Don't make noises at me! Don't look at me! Don't do anything. *(telephone business, swiftly)* Hello, g'bye! *(He disappears.)*

TOMMY. Moe!…Moe!…Talk to me something!…Moe, why are you that way at me?

MOE. *(surging up again, glaring)* My daddy says I'm stupid. He says, "Stupid, come here!" He says, "All right, stupid, fall down!" I don't want to talk. I don't want to look. G'bye!

(He disappears.)

TOMMY. What does "stupid" mean?

MOE. *(invisible)* I won't tell. *(surging up, showing his fingers; a rapid-fire jumble)* Do you know what these are? Sometimes you call them fingers; sometimes you call them piggies. One, two, six, five, four, two, ten. This little piggie stayed at home, I don't know why that is. Do you know what you do when the loud bell rings? You do this: *(telephone business)* "Hello...jugga...jugga... jugga," and when you don't like it any more you say, "G'bye!" Maybe I am stupid. – But that's because MY MOUTH HURTS ALL THE TIME and they don't give me enough to eat and I'm hungry all the time and that's the end of it, that's the end of it.

(He disappears.)

TOMMY. Moe, tell me some more things.

MOE. *(surging up again)* "Stupid, come here!" "Stupid, get your goddamn tail out of here!" *(shaking his carriage)* I hate him. I hate him. But I watch him and I learn. *You see*: I learn. And when I get to walk I'm going to do something so that he won't *be* any more. He'll be away – away where people can walk on him. – Don't you hate your father?

TOMMY. Well...I don't see him much. Like, once a year.

MOE. You mean: once a day.

TOMMY. Moe, what does "year" mean?

MOE. Year is when it's cold.

TOMMY. *(brightening)* Yes, I know.

MOE. Sometimes he holds out his hands and says: "How's the little fella? How's the little champ?" And I give him a look! I wasn't born yesterday. He hasn't got anything to sell to me.

TOMMY. Moe – where's your mommy? *(silence)* Moe, she's not here. Where's your mommy? You don't hate your mommy, do you?

MOE. *(turning his face sideways, cold and proud)* I don't care about her. She's always away. She goes away for years. She laughs at me...with that *man*. He says: "All right, fall down, stupid," and she laughs. I try to talk to her and she goes away all the time and does, "Hello – jugga – jugga-jugga-goo-bye!" If she don't care about me any more, I don't care about her any more. Goo-bye! *(silence)*

TOMMY. Say some more, Moe, say some more things.

MOE. *(low and intense)* Maybe I am stupid. Maybe I'll never be able to walk or make talk. Maybe they didn't give me good feet or a good mouth. – You know what I think? I think they don't want us to walk and to get good and get better. They want us to *stop*. That's what I think. *(His voice has risen to a hysterical wail.)* Goddam! Hell! *(He starts throwing cloth elephants and giraffes out of the carriage.)* I'm not going to try. Nobody wants to help me and lots of time is passing and I'm not getting bigger, and...and... *(anticlimax)* I'm sleepeee... *(He continues to whimper.)*

(MILLIE wakes up. She goes gingerly to MOE's carriage and joggles it.)

MILLIE. Moe! What's the matter, Moe? "Rockabye, baby, in the treetop – "

(MOE wails more loudly.)

Oh, goodness, gracious me. *(in desperation)* Moe! Do you know that *that* street is called Central Park West? And then there's Columbus Avenue? And then there's Amsterdam Avenue? And then there's Broadway?

(MOE has hushed.)

And then there's West End Avenue. *(She can hardly believe her luck; she whispers:)* And then there's Riverside Drive. *(She peers into the carriage a long time, then tiptoes to the other end of the stage; with clenched fists.)* I hate babies. *(toward TOMMY)* I hate you – sticking your crazy face into my business – frightening Officer Avonzino, the only man I've talked to in six months. I hate you – always butting in. I have a right to my own life, haven't I? *My own life!* I'm sick to death of squall-ing, smelling, gawking babies…I'd be a stenographer only I don't know anything; nobody ever taught me anything… "Manhattan, the Bronx" – what do I care what keeps you quiet? You can yell your heads off for all I care! I don't know why nature didn't make it so that people came into the world already grown-up – instead of a dozen and more years of screaming and diapers and falling down and breaking everything… and asking questions! "What's that?" "Why-y-y?" "Why-y-y?"…Officer Avonzino will never come back, that's certain!…Oh, what do I care? You're going to grow up to be men – nasty, selfish men. You're all alike.

(Drying her eyes, she picks up her novel from **TOMMY***'s carriage and strolls off the stage at the back.)*

*(***MOE***'s head, now solemn and resolute, rises slowly.)*

MOE. Tommy!…Tommy!

TOMMY. *(appearing)* I'm tired.

MOE. You know what I'm going to do, do you?

TOMMY. No – what, Moe?

MOE. I'm just going to lie still.

TOMMY. What do you mean, Moe?

MOE. I'll shut my eyes and do nothing. I won't eat. I'll just go away-away. Like I want Daddy to do.

TOMMY. *(alarm)* No, Moe! Don't go where people can walk on you!

MOE. Well, I *will*…You know what I think? I think people aren't SERIOUS about us. "Little piggie went to market, cradle will fall, Manhattan, the Bronx" – that's not serious. They don't want us to get better.

TOMMY. *Maybe* they do.

MOE. Old people are only interested in old people. Like kiss-kiss-kiss; that's all they do; that's all they think about.

TOMMY. *(eagerly)* Ye-e-es! Miss'a Millie, all the time, kiss-kiss-kiss, but she don't mean me; she means the policerman.

MOE. We're in the way, see? We're too little, that's how. I don't want to be a man – it's too hard!

(He disappears.)

TOMMY. *(with increasing alarm)* Moe!…Moe!…Don't stop talking, Moe!…MOE!

*(**MILLIE** returns hastily)*

MILLIE. Now what's the matter with you? I'll spank you. Always crying and making a baby of yourself.

TOMMY. *(at the same time; frantic)* Moe's going away-away. He's not going to eat any more. Go look at Moe…*Do* something. *Do* something!

MILLIE. What is the matter with you? Why can't you be quiet like Moe? *(She goes and looks in **MOE**'s carriage and is terrified by what she sees.)* Help!…Hellllp! The baby's turned purple! Moe! Have you swallowed something? – *(She dashes to the audience exit.)* Officer Avonzino! Officer! Hellllp! – Oh, they'll kill me. What'll I do?

*(**OFFICER AVONZINO** rushes in from the audience.)*

AVONZINO. What'a matter, Miss Wilchick; you gone crazy today?

MILLIE. *(gasping)* …look…he's turned black, Officer Avonzino…His mother's over at the museum. Oh…I don't know what to do.

*(**OFFICER AVONZINO**, efficient but unhurried, opens his tunic and takes out his handbook. He hunts for the correct page.)*

AVONZINO. First, don't scream, Miss Wilchick. Nobody scream. Babies die every day. Always new babies. Nothing to scream about…Babies turn black – so! Babies turn blue, black, purple, all the time. Hmph "Turn baby over, lift middle…" *(He does these things.)* "Water…" *(to **MILLIE**)* Go to nurses over there…twenty nurses…Bring back some ippycack.

MILLIE. Oh, Officer…help me. I'm fainting.

AVONZINO. *(furious)* Faintings on *Sundays* – not workdays, Miss Wilchick.

MILLIE. *(hand to head)* Oh...oh...

(OFFICER AVONZINO catches her just in time and drapes her over the bench like a puppet.)

AVONZINO. "Lesson Thirty-Two: Let Mother Die. Save Baby." I get water. *(he dashes off)*

(TOMMY raises his head)

TOMMY. Moe! Don't be black. Don't be black. You're going to walk soon. And by and by you can go to school. And even if they don't teach you good, you can kind of teach yourself.

(MOE is sobbing)

Moe, what's that noise you're making? Make a crying like a baby, Moe. – Soon you can be big and shave. And be a policeman. And you can make kiss-kiss-kiss...and make babies. And, Moe –

MOE. *(appearing)* Don't talk to me. I'm tired. I'm tired.

TOMMY. And you can show your babies how to walk and talk.

MOE. *(yawning)* I'm...tire'... *(he sinks back)*

TOMMY. *(yawning)* I'm tired, tooooo. *(he sinks back)*

(OFFICER AVONZINO returns with a child's pail of water. He leans over MOE.)

AVONZINO. *(astonished)* What'a matter with you!! You all red again. You not sick. Goddamn! Tricks. Babies always doing tricks. *(shakes MILLIE)* Miss Wilchick! Wake up! Falsa alarm. Baby's okay.

MILLIE. *(coming to, dreamily)* Oh, Officer... *(extending her arms amorously)* Oh you're so...handsome...Officer...

AVONZINO. *(sternly)* "Lesson Eleven: No Personal Remarks with Public." *(shouts)* It's going to rain: better take George Washington home...and Dr. Einstein, too.

MILLIE. Oh! How *is* the Boker baby?

AVONZINO. Boker baby's a great actor. Dies every performance. Thousands cheer.

MILLIE. *(pushes* **TOMMY** *toward exit)* Oh, I can't go until Mrs. Boker comes back.

(peers out) – Oh, there she comes, running. See her?

AVONZINO. You *go*. I take care of baby til a'momma comes.

(At exit **MILLIE** *turns for a heartfelt farewell; he points billy stick and commands her.)*

Go *faint*, Miss Wilchick!

(She goes out. **OFFICER AVONZINO** *addresses* **MOE.***)*

I'd like to make your damn bottom red. I know you. All you babies want the whole world. Well, I tell you, you've got a long hard road before you. Pretty soon you'll find that you can cry all you want and turn every color there is – and nobody'll pay *no* attention at all. Your best days are over; you've had'm. From now on it's all up to you – George Washington, or whatever your name is.

(enter **MRS. BOKER**, *breathless)*

MRS. BOKER. Oh!!

AVONZINO. I sent Miss Wilchick home. *(pointing toward rain)* You better start off yourself.

MRS. BOKER. *(pushing the carriage to the exit)* Has everything been all right, Officer?

AVONZINO. Just fine, lady, just fine. Like usual: babies acting like growed-ups; growed-ups acting like babies.

MRS. BOKER. Thank you, Officer.

(She goes out.)

*(***OFFICER AVONZINO**, *shading his eyes, peers down the aisle through the audience. Suddenly he sees something that outrages him. Like a Keystone cop he does a double take and starts running through the audience, shouting.)*

AVONZINO. Hey there!! You leave that baby carriage alone! Don't you know what's inside them baby carriages?...

End of Play

CHILDHOOD

A Comedy

CHARACTERS

CAROLINE, the oldest daughter, twelve
DODIE, her sister, ten
BILLEE, her brother, eight
MOTHER
FATHER

SETTING

A suburban house and yard.

(Some low chairs at the edges of the arena. These at first represent some bushes in the yard of the children's home. At the back, the door to the house; the aisle through the audience serves as a path to the street. Enter from the house **CAROLINE**, *twelve;* **DODIE**, *ten; and, with a rush,* **BILLEE**, *eight.)*

DODIE. Shh! Shh! Don't let Mama hear you! Car'line, Car'line, play the game. Let's play the game.

CAROLINE. There's no time, silly. It takes time to play the game.

BILLEE. Play Goin' to China.

CAROLINE. Don't talk so loud; we don't want Mama to hear us. Papa'll be here soon, and we can't play the game when Papa's here.

DODIE. Well, let's play a little. We can play Going to a Hotel.

BILLEE. *(clamorously)* I want to be Room Service. I want to be Room Service.

CAROLINE. You know Going to a Hotel takes *hours*. It's awful when you have to stop for something.

DODIE. *(quickly)* Car'line, listen, I heard Mama telephoning Papa and the car's got to be fixed and Papa's got to come home by a bus, and maybe he'll never get here and we can play for a long time.

CAROLINE. Did she say that? Well, come behind the bushes and think.

(They squat on their haunches behind the bushes.)

BILLEE. Let's play Hospital and take everything out of Dodie.

CAROLINE. Let me think a minute.

MOTHER. *(at the door)* Caroline! Dodie! *(silence)* Dodie, how often do I have to tell you to hang your coat up properly? Do you know what happened? It fell and got caught under the cupboard door and was dragged back and forth. I hope it's warm Sunday, because you can't wear that coat. Billee, stand out for a moment where I can see you. Are you ready for your father when he comes home? Come out of the bushes, Billee, come out.

(**BILLEE**, *a stoic already, comes to the center of the stage and stands for inspection.* **MOTHER** *shakes her head in silence; then:*)

I simply despair. Look at you! What are you children doing anyway? Now, Caroline, you're not playing one of those games of yours? I absolutely forbid you to play that the house is on fire. You have nightmares all night long. Or those awful games about hospitals. Really, Caroline, why can't you play Shopping or Going to School? *(silence)* I declare. I give up. I really do. *(false exit)* Now remember, it's Friday night, the end of the week, and you give your father a good big kiss when he comes home.

(She goes out.)

(**BILLEE** *rejoins his sisters.*)

DODIE. *(dramatic whisper)* Car'line, let's play Funeral! *(climax)* Car'line, let's play ORPHANS!

CAROLINE. We haven't time – *that* takes all day. Besides, I haven't got the black gloves.

(**BILLEE** *sees his* **FATHER** *coming through the audience. Utter and final dismay.*)

BILLEE. Look't! Look!

DODIE. What?

ALL THREE. It's Papa! It's Papa!

(They fly into the house like frightened pigeons. **FATHER** *enters jauntily through the audience. It's warm, and he carries his coat over his shoulder. Arriving at the center of the stage, he places his coat on the ground, whistles a signal call to his wife, and swinging an imaginary golf club, executes a mighty and very successful shot.)*

FATHER. Two hundred and fifty yards!

MOTHER. (*enters, kisses him and picks up the coat*) Why, you're early, after all.

FATHER. Jerry drove me to the corner. Picked up a little flask for the weekend.

MOTHER. Well, I wish you wouldn't open your little flask when the children are around.

FATHER. (*preparing a difficult shot*) Eleventh hole...Where *are* the children?

MOTHER. They were here a minute ago. They're out playing somewhere...Your coat on the ground! Really, you're as bad as Dodie.

FATHER. Well, you should teach the children – little trouble with the dandelions here – that it's their first duty... when their father comes home on Friday nights... (*shouts*) Fore, you bastards!...to rush toward their father...to grovel...abject thanks to him who gave them life.

MOTHER. (*amused exasperation*) Oh, stop that nonsense!

FATHER. On Friday nights...after a week of toil at the office...a man wants to see... (*He swings.*) his wives and children clinging to his knees, tears pouring down their cheeks. (*He stands up very straight, holding an enormous silver cup.*) Gentlemen, I accept this championship cup, but I wish also to give credit to my wife and children, who drove me out of the house every Sunday morning... Where *are* the children? Caroline! Dodie!

MOTHER. Oh, they're hiding somewhere.

FATHER. Hiding? Hiding from their father?

MOTHER. They're playing one of those awful games of theirs. Listen to me, Fred – those games are morbid; they're dangerous.

FATHER. How do you mean, dangerous?

MOTHER. Really! No one told me when I was a bride that children are half crazy. I only hear fragments of the games, naturally, but do you realize that they like nothing better than to imagine us – away?

FATHER. Away?

MOTHER. Yes – dead?

FATHER. *(his eye on the shot)* One…two…*three!* Well, you know what *you* said.

MOTHER. What did I say?

FATHER. *Your* dream.

MOTHER. Pshaw!

FATHER. *(softly, with lowest insinuation)* Your dream that… you and I…on a Mediterranean cruise…

MOTHER. It was Hawaii.

FATHER. And that we were – ahem! – somehow…*alone.*

MOTHER. Well, I didn't imagine them *dead!* I imagined them with Mother…or Paul…or their Aunt Henrietta.

FATHER. *(piously)* I hope so.

MOTHER. You're a brute, and everybody knows it…It's Caroline. She's the one who starts it all. And afterwards she has those nightmares. Come in. You'll see the children at supper.

FATHER. *(looking upward)* What has the weatherman predicted for tomorrow?

MOTHER. *(starting for the house)* Floods. Torrents. You're going to stay home from the golf club and take care of the children. And I'm going to the Rocky Mountains… and to China.

FATHER. You'll be back by noon. What does Caroline say in her nightmares?

MOTHER. Oh! When she's awake, too. You and I are – away. Do you realize that that girl is mad about black gloves?

FATHER. Nonsense.

MOTHER. Caroline would be in constant mourning if she could manage it. Come in, come in. You'll see them at supper.

(She goes out.)

FATHER. *(He strolls to the end of the stage farthest from the house and calls.)* Caroline! *(pause)* Dodie! *(pause)* Bill-eeee!

(Silence. He broods aloud, his eyes on the distance.)

FATHER. No instrument has yet been discovered that can read what goes on in another's mind, asleep or awake. And I hope there never will be. But once in a while, it would help a lot. Is it wrong of me to wish that…just once…I could be an invisible witness to one of my children's dreams, to one of their games? *(He calls again.)* Caroline!

(We are in the game which is a dream. The children enter as he calls them, but he does not see them and they do not see him. They come in and stand shoulder to shoulder as though they were about to sing a song before an audience. **CAROLINE** *carries a child's suitcase and one of her* **MOTHER**'s *handbags; she is wearing black gloves.* **DODIE** *also has a suitcase and handbag, but no gloves)*

CAROLINE. Dodie! Hurry before they see us.

FATHER. Dodie!

DODIE. Where's Billee gone?

FATHER. *(being bumped into by* **BILLEE** *as he joins his sisters)* Billee!

*(***FATHER** *enters the house.* **MOTHER** *glides out of the house and takes her place at the farther end of the stage and turns and faces the children. She is wearing a black hat, deep black veil and black gloves. Her air is one of mute acquiescent grief.* **CAROLINE** *glances frequently at her* **MOTHER** *as though for prompting. A slight formal pause.)*

CAROLINE. I guess, first, we have to say how sorry we are. *(to* **MOTHER**) Shall we begin? *(***MOTHER** *lowers her head slightly.)* This first part is in church. Well, in a kind of church. And there's been a perfectly terrible accident, an airplane accident.

DODIE. *(quickly)* No, it was an automobile accident.

CAROLINE. *(ditto)* It was an airplane.

DODIE. *(ditto)* I don't want it to be an airplane.

BILLEE. *(fiercely)* It was on a ship. It was a *big* shipwreck.

CAROLINE. Now, I'm not going to play this game unless you be quiet. It was an airplane accident. And…They were on it, and they're not here any more.

BILLEE. They got *dead*.

CAROLINE. *(glaring at him)* Don't say that *word*. You promised you wouldn't say that word. *(uncomfortable pause)* And we're very sad. And…

DODIE. *(brightly)* We didn't see it, though.

CAROLINE. And we'd have put on black dresses, only we haven't got any. But we want to thank Miss Wilkerson for coming today and for wearing black like she's wearing. (**MOTHER** *again lowers her head.*) Miss Wilkerson is the best teacher in Benjamin Franklin School, and she's the grown-up we like best.

BILLEE. *(suddenly getting excited)* That's not Miss Wilkerson. That's – I mean – *look!*

CAROLINE. I can't hear a word you're saying, and anyway, don't talk now!

BILLEE. *(too young to enter the dream; pulling at his sisters' sleeves urgently)* That's not Miss Wilkerson. That's *Mama!*

DODIE. What's the matter with your eyes?

CAROLINE. Mama's not here any more. She went away.

BILLEE. *(staring at* **MOTHER,** *and beginning to doubt)* It's… Mrs. Fenwick!

CAROLINE. *(low but strongly)* No-o-o-o! *(resuming the ceremony)* It wasn't so sad about Grandma, because she was more'n a hundred anyway.

DODIE. And she used to say all the time, "I won't be with you always," and things like that, and how she'd give Mama her pearl pin.

BILLEE. I guess she's glad she isn't any more.

CAROLINE. *(uncertainly)* So…

DODIE. *(to* **MOTHER,** *with happy excitement)* Are we orphans now – real orphans? (**MOTHER,** *always with lowered eyes, nods slightly.*) And we don't have to *do things* any more?

CAROLINE. *(severely)* Dodie! Don't *say* everything. *(She consults her* **MOTHER.***)* What do I say now?

MOTHER. *(almost inaudibly)* About your father...

CAROLINE. Yes. Papa was a very fine man. And...

DODIE. *(quickly)* He used to swear bad words.

BILLEE. *(excitedly)* All the *time!* He'd swear swearwords.

CAROLINE. Well, maybe a little.

DODIE. He *did. I* used to want to *die.*

CAROLINE. Well, nobody's perfect. *(slower)* He was all right, sometimes.

DODIE. He used to laugh too loud in front of people. And he didn't give Mama enough money to buy clothes. She had to go to town in rags, in terrible old rags.

BILLEE. *(always excited)* Papa'd go like this, *(pumping his arms up and down in desperation)* "I haven't got it! I haven't got it! You can't squeeze blood out of a stone."

DODIE. Yes, he did.

BILLEE. And Mama'd say: "I'm ashamed to go out in the street." It was awful. And then he'd say, "I'll have to mortgage, that's what I'll have to do."

CAROLINE. Billee! How can you say such an awful word? Don't you ever say that again. Papa wasn't perfect, but he would never have done a mortgage.

BILLEE. Well, that's what he said.

CAROLINE. *(emphatically)* Most times Papa did his best. Everybody makes some mistakes.

DODIE. *(demurely)* He used to drink some, too.

BILLEE. *(beside himself again)* He used to drink *oceans.* And Mama'd say, "Don't you think you've had enough?" and he'd say, "Down the hatch!"

DODIE. Yes, he did. And, "Just a hair of the dog that bit him." And Mama'd say, "Well, if you want to kill yourself before our eyes!" I used to want to die.

CAROLINE. Billee, don't get so excited; and you too, Dodie. Papa was a very fine man, and he *tried.* Only...only... *(reluctantly)* he didn't ever say anything very interesting.

DODIE. He was interesting when he told about the automobile accident he'd seen and all the blood.

BILLEE. Yes, he was. But he stopped in the middle when Mama said, "Not before the children."

DODIE. Yes, he stopped then.

CAROLINE. Anyway, we're very sad. And…

(She looks to her MOTHER for prompting.)

MOTHER. *(almost inaudibly)* Your mother…

CAROLINE. Yes. About Mama.

BILLEE. *(hot indignation)* Mama's almost never home. She's always shopping and having her hair made. And one time she was away *years*, to see Grandma in Boston.

DODIE. It was only five days, and Grandma was very sick.

BILLEE. No, it wasn't. It was years and years.

DODIE. Well, when she was away she didn't have to say Don't-Don't-Don't all the time, all day and night, Don't-Don't-Don't.

BILLEE. *(tentatively defending her)* Sometimes she makes good things to eat.

DODIE. Beans and mash potatoes, and I just hate them. "Now, you eat every mouthful, or you don't leave the table." Ugh!

CAROLINE. *(recalling them to the ceremony)* It wasn't her fault! Only she didn't unnerstand children. I guess there's not one in a hundred hundred that understands children. *(to MOTHER)* Is that enough, Miss Wilkerson? I can't think of anything else to say. And we've got to hurry, or Uncle Paul will come to get us, or Aunt Henrietta, or somebody even worse. So can we go now?

MOTHER. *(a whisper)* I think it would be nice, you know, if you said how you loved them, and how they loved you.

CAROLINE. Yes – uh…

DODIE. It was awful when they got huggy and kissy. And when we got back an hour late, from Mary Louise's picnic, and Mama said, "I was frantic! I was frantic! I didn't know what had become of you."

CAROLINE. *(slowly)* She liked us best when we were sick and when I broke my arm.

DODIE. Yes. *(exhausted pause)* Miss Wilkerson, orphans don't have to be sad *all* the time, do they?

*(**MOTHER** shakes her head slightly.)*

BILLEE. Do we get any money for being orphans?

CAROLINE. We won't need it. Papa used to keep an envelope behind the clock with money in it, for accidents and times like that. I have it here. *(She goes to **MOTHER**, like a hostess getting rid of a guest.)* Thank you for coming, Miss Wilkerson. We have to go now. And thank you for wearing black.

DODIE. *(also shaking hands; conventionally)* Thank you very much.

*(**MOTHER**, with bowed head, glides into the house.)*

CAROLINE. Now be quiet, and I'll tell you what we're going to do. We've got to hurry, so don't interrupt me. We're orphans and we don't have anybody around us or near us and we're going to take a bus.

(sensation) All over the world. We're going to be different persons and we're going to change our names. *(Gravely she opens her suitcase. She takes out and puts on a hat and fur neckpiece of her **MOTHER**'s. She looks adorable.)* I'm Mrs. Arizona. Miss Wilson, please get ready for the trip.

DODIE. Wha-a-t?

CAROLINE. *Miss Wilson!* Will you put your hat on, please.

DODIE. Oh! *(She puts on a hat from her suitcase.)* I want to be married, too. I want to be Mrs. Wilson.

CAROLINE. You're too young. People would laugh at you. We'll be gone for years and years, and by and by, in China or somewhere, you can gradually be Mrs. Wilson.

BILLEE. I want to be somebody, too.

CAROLINE. You're only *eight!* If you don't cry all the time and say awful things, I'll give you a real name. Now we can start.

BILLEE. But aren't Papa and Mama coming?

(The girls turn and glare at him.)

Ooh! they're *dead. (more glaring)*

CAROLINE. All right. S-s-stay at home and go to s-s-school, if you want to. Papa and Mama are *happy*. Papa's playing golf and Mama's shopping. Are you ready, Miss Wilson?

DODIE. Yes, Mrs. Arizona, thank you.

CAROLINE. Don't run, but if we hurry we can each get a seat by the window.

(FATHER enters, wearing a bus conductor's cap and big dark glasses. He casually arranges the chairs so as to indicate some of the seats of a long bus pointing toward the exit through the audience. The children form a line at the door of the bus, tickets in hand.)

FATHER. Take your places in line, please. The first stop, ladies and gentlemen, will be Ashagorra-Kallapalla, where there will be twenty minutes for lunch. That's the place where you get to eat the famous heaven-fruit sandwich. *(He starts punching the tickets of some imaginary passengers who precede the children.)* That cat won't be happy, madam. That's our experience. *(severely, palping a passenger)* You haven't got mumps, have you? Well, I'd appreciate it if you sat at a distance from the other passengers.

BILLEE. *(staggered)* But that's Papa!

DODIE. Don't be silly, Papa's *away*.

BILLEE. But it looks like Papa...and... *(losing assurance)* it looks like Dr. Summers, too.

CAROLINE. Billee, I don't know what's the matter with you. Papa wouldn't be working as a bus conductor. Papa's a man that's got more money than that.

FATHER. *(to CAROLINE)* Your ticket, please, madam.

CAROLINE. We want to go to all the places you're going to, please.

FATHER. But you mean this to be a round-trip ticket, don't you? You're coming back, aren't you?

CAROLINE. *(none too sure; her eyes avoiding his)* Well, maybe I won't.

FATHER. *(lowering his voice, confidentially)* I'll punch it on the side here. That'll mean you can use it, whenever you want, to come back here.

(CAROLINE takes her place on the bus.)

(MOTHER glides in and takes her place in the line behind BILLEE. She is now wearing a brown hat and a deep brown veil. FATHER punches DODIE's ticket.)

Why, I think. I've seen your face before, madam. Weren't you in that terrible automobile accident – blood all over the road and everything?

DODIE. *(embarrassed; low)* No, no, I wasn't.

FATHER. Well, I'm glad to hear that.

(DODIE takes her seat behind CAROLINE.)

(to BILLEE, punching his ticket) And what's your name, sir, if I may ask?

BILLEE. Billee.

CAROLINE. *(officiously)* His name is Mr. Wentworth.

FATHER. Mr. Wentworth. Good morning.

(man to man, with a touch of severity) No smoking in the first six rows, watch that, and...

(significant whisper) there'll be no liquor drinking on this bus. I hope that's understood.

(BILLEE, considerably intimidated, takes his place behind DODIE. During the following he sees MOTHER and stares at her in amazement.)

(FATHER punches MOTHER's ticket, saying in sad condolence:)

I hope you have a good trip, ma'am. I hope you have a good trip.

MOTHER. *(a whisper)* Thank you.

(She takes a place in the last row.)

CAROLINE. *(rummaging in her handbag)* Would you like a candy bar, Miss Wilson...and Mr. Wentworth?

DODIE. Thank you, Mrs. Arizona, I would.

BILLEE. Look! LOOK! That's Mama!

DODIE. Stop poking me. It's not. It's *not*.

FATHER. Well, now, all aboard that's going to go.

(He climbs on the bus, takes his seat, tries his gears, then rises and addresses the passengers weightily.) Before we start, there are some things I want to say about this trip. *Bus travel is not easy.* I think you'll know what I mean, Mrs. Arizona, when I say that it's like family life – we're all stuck in this vehicle together. We go through some pretty dangerous country, and I want you all to keep your heads. Like when we go through the Black Snake Indian territory, for instance. I've just heard they're getting a little – restless. And along the Kappikappi River, where all those lions and tigers are, and other things. Now, I'm a pretty good driver, but nobody's perfect and everybody can make a mistake once in a while. But I don't want any complaints afterward that you weren't warned. If anybody wants to get off this bus and go home, this is the moment to do it, and I'll give you your money back.

(indicating **MOTHER***)* There's one passenger here I know can be counted on. She's made the trip before and she's a regular crackerjack. Excuse me praising you to your face, ma'am, but I mean every word of it. Now, how many of you have been trained in first aid – will you hold up your hands?

*(***BILLEE*** and* **MOTHER*** raise their hands promptly.* **CAROLINE*** and* **DODIE*** look at one another uncertainly but do not raise their hands.)*

Well, we may have to hold some classes later – go to school, so to speak. Accidents are always likely to happen when we get to the tops of the mountains. So! I guess we're ready to start. When we start, we often have a word of prayer if there's a minister of the gospel on board. *(to* **BILLEE***)* May I ask if you're a minister of the gospel, Mr. Wentworth?

BILLEE. N-no.

FATHER. Then we'll just have to *think* it. *(lowering his voice, to* **BILLEE***)* And, may I add, I hope that there won't be any bad language used on this bus. There are ladies present – and some very fine ladies, too, if I may say so. Well, here we go! Forward march.

CAROLINE. *(to* **DODIE***, confidentially)* If it's going to be so dangerous, I think we'd better move up a little nearer *him*.

(They slip across the aisle and slide, side by side, into the second row behind **FATHER***.* **BILLEE** *has gone to the back of the car and stands staring at* **MOTHER***.)*

BILLEE. *(indicating the veil)* Do you ever take that off?

MOTHER. *(softly, lowered eyes)* Sometimes I do.

CAROLINE. Billee! Don't disturb the lady. Come and sit by us.

MOTHER. Oh, he's not disturbing me at all.

(Soon he takes the seat beside her, and she puts her arm around him.)

FATHER. *(as he drives, talking to the girls over his shoulder)* It's hard work driving a bus, ladies. Did you ever think of that?

CAROLINE. Oh, yes. It must be hard.

FATHER. Sometimes I wonder why I do it. Mornings...leave my house and family and get on the bus. And it's no fun, believe me. *(jerk)* See that? Almost ran over that soldier. And – would you believe it – I don't get much money for it.

CAROLINE. *(breathless interest)* Don't they pay you a *lot?*

FATHER. Mrs. Arizona, I'm telling you the truth – sometimes I wonder if we're going to have enough to eat.

DODIE. Why, I think that's terrible!

FATHER. And if I can get enough clothes to wear. I see that's a nice fur piece you have on, Mrs. Arizona.

CAROLINE. Oh, this is *old*.

DODIE. *(very earnestly)* But at your house you do have breakfast and lunch and supper, don't you?

FATHER. Miss Wilson, you're awfully kind to ask. So far we have. Sometimes it's just, you know, beans and things like that. Life's not easy, Mrs. Arizona. You must have noticed that.

BILLEE. *(big alarm)* Mr. Bus Conductor, look't. Look over there!

FATHER. *(galvanized; all stare toward the left)* Ladies and gentlemen, there are those goldarn Indians again! I want you to put your heads right down on the floor! Right down!

(All except **FATHER** *crouch on the floor:)*

I don't want any of them arrows to come in the windows and hit you. (**FATHER** *fires masterfully from the hip.)* They'll be sorry for this. BANG! BANG! That'll teach them. BANG!

*(***BILLEE*** *rises and whirls, shooting splendidly in all directions.)*

There! The danger's over, ladies and gentlemen. You can get in your seats now. I'll report that to the Man Up There in Washington, D.C., you see if I don't. *(to* **MOTHER***)* May I ask if you're all right back there?

MOTHER. Yes, thank you, Mr. Bus Conductor. I want to say that Mr. Wentworth behaved splendidly. I don't think that I'd be here except for him.

FATHER. Good! Minute I saw him I knew he had the old stuff in him! Ladies, I think you did A-number-one, too.

CAROLINE. Does that happen often, Mr. Bus Conductor?

FATHER. Well, you know what a man's life is like, Mrs. Arizona. Fight. Struggle. Survive. Struggle. Survive. Always was.

DODIE. What if – what if you *didn't* come back?

FATHER. Do you mean, if I died? We don't think of that, Miss Wilson. But when we come home Friday nights we like to see the look on the faces of our wives and children. Another week, and we're still there. And do you know what I do on my free days, Miss Wilson, after sitting cooped up behind this wheel?

DODIE. *(sudden inspiration)* Play golf.

FATHER. You're bright, Miss Wilson, bright as a penny.

CAROLINE. *(who has been glancing at **MOTHER**)* Mr. Bus Conductor, can I ask you why that lady – why she's so sad?

FATHER. You don't know?

CAROLINE. No.

FATHER. *(lowering his voice)* She just got some bad news. Her children left the house.

CAROLINE. Did they?

FATHER. Don't mention it to her, will you?

CAROLINE. *(insecurely)* Why did they do that?

FATHER. Well, children are funny. Funny. Now I come to think of it, it'd be nice if, a little later, you went back and sort of comforted her. Like Mr. Wentworth's doing.

DODIE. Wasn't she good to them?

FATHER. What's that?

DODIE. Wasn't she a *good* mother?

FATHER. Well, let me ask *you* a question: is there any such thing as a good mother or a good father? Look at me: I do the best I can for my family – things to eat, you know, and dresses and shoes. I see you've got some real pretty shoes on, ladies. But, well, *children don't understand,* and that's all you can say about it. Do you know what one of my daughters said to me last week? She said she wished she was an orphan. Hard. Very hard.

CAROLINE. *(struggling)* Lots of times parents don't understand children, either.

FATHER. *(abruptly breaking the mood)* But now, ladies and gentlemen, I have a treat for you. *(Stops the bus and points dramatically to the front right. All gaze in awe.)* Isn't that a sight! The Mississippi River! Isn't that a lot of water!

MOTHER. *(after a moment's gaze, with increasing concern)* But-but-Mr. Bus Conductor.

FATHER. *(looking back at her and sharing her anxiety)* Madam, I think I know what you're thinking, and it troubles me too. (**MOTHER** *has come halfway down the aisle, her eyes on the river.*) Ladies and gentlemen, the river's in flood. I don't think I've ever seen it so high. The question is: would it be safe to cross it today? Look yourselves – would that bridge hold?

MOTHER. *(returning to her seat)* Mr. Bus Conductor, may I make a suggestion?

FATHER. You certainly may.

MOTHER. I suggest that you ask the passengers to raise their hands if they think it's best that we don't cross the Mississippi today.

FATHER. *Very* good idea! That'll mean we turn around and go back to where we came from. Now think it over, ladies and gentlemen. All who are ready to do that raise their hands.

*(****MOTHER**** and ****BILLEE**** raise their hands at once. Then* **DODIE.** *Finally, unhappily,* **CAROLINE.** **FATHER** *earnestly counts the twenty hands in the bus.)*

All right! Everybody wants to go back. So, here we go. *(He starts the bus.)* Now, I'm going to go pretty fast, so sit square in your seats.

(after a pause, confidentially over his shoulder to **CAROLINE***)* I hope you really meant it when you put your hand up, Mrs. Arizona.

CAROLINE. Well…

FATHER. You *do* have some folks waiting for you at home, don't you?

DODIE. *(quickly)* Yes, we do.

CAROLINE. *(slowly, near to tears)* But we didn't get to China or to that river where the lions and tigers are. It's too soon to go back to where I come from, where everybody says silly things they don't mean one bit, and where nobody treats you like a real person. And we didn't get to eat the famous heaven-fruit sandwich at that place.

DODIE. *(embarrassed)* Car'line, you can do it another time.

*(**CAROLINE**'s lowered head shows that she doesn't believe this.)*

FATHER. *(confidentially)* Mrs. Arizona, I'll honor that ticket *at any time,* and I'll be looking for you.

CAROLINE. *(raises her eyes to him gravely; after a minute she says, also in a low voice)* Mr. Bus Conductor –

FATHER. Yes, Mrs. Arizona.

CAROLINE. Do you get paid just the same, even if you didn't go the whole way?

FATHER. I? Oh, don't you think of that, ma'am. We can tighten our belts. There's always something.

CAROLINE. *(groping feverishly in her handbag, with a quick sob)* No! I haven't got a *lot* of money, but – here! Here's more' n two dollars, and you can buy a lot of things to eat with that.

FATHER. *(quietly and slowly, his eyes on the road)* That's real thoughtful of you, Mrs. Arizona, and I thank you. But you put that away and keep it. I feel sure that this is going to be my good year. *(after a pause)* Excuse me, may I put my hand on your hand a minute to show you know I appreciate what you did?

CAROLINE. *(shy)* Yes, you may.

(He does so, very respectfully; then returns to his wheel.)

DODIE. Car'line, what're you crying about?

CAROLINE. When...you try to *do* something for some-body...and...

FATHER. *(very cheerful and loud)* Gee whillikers! My wife will be surprised to see me back home so soon. Poor old thing, she doesn't have many pleasures. Just a little shopping now and then. *(He tosses off a snatch of song.)* "The son of a, son of a, son of a gambolier..." I think this would be a good time to go back and say a nice word to that lady who's had a little disappointment in her home, don't you?

CAROLINE. Well, uh…Come, Dodie.

(CAROLINE *goes back and sits in front of* MOTHER, *talking to her over the back of the seat;* DODIE *stands beside her.*)

The bus conductor says that everybody isn't in your house any more.

MOTHER. *(lowered eyes)* Did he? That's true.

CAROLINE. They'll come back. I know they will.

MOTHER. Oh, do you think so?

CAROLINE. Children don't like being treated as children *all the time.* And I think it isn't worthwhile being born into the world if you have to do the same things every day.

DODIE. The reason I don't like grown-ups is that they don't ever think any interesting thoughts. I guess they're so old that they just get tired of expecting anything to be different or exciting. So they just do the same old golfing and shopping.

CAROLINE. *(suddenly seeing a landmark through the window)* Mr. Bus Conductor! Mr. Bus Conductor! Please, will you please stop at the next corner? This is where we have to get off. *(under her voice, commandingly)* Come, Dodie, Billee. Come quick!

(*They start up the aisle toward the bus exit, then turn back to* MOTHER. *Their farewells are their best party manners.*)

THE CHILDREN. *(shaking hands with both parents)* I'm very glad to have met you. Thank you very much. I'm very glad to have met you.

FATHER. *(as* MOTHER *joins him at the bus exit)* But you'll come on my bus again? We'll see you again?

CAROLINE. *(to* DODIE *and* BILLEE, *low)* Now, run!

(*They run into the house like rabbits. She stands at the bus door, with lowered eyes.*)

Well…you see…you're just people in our game. You're not *really* alive. That's why we could talk to you.

CAROLINE. *(a quick glance at her* **FATHER**, *then she looks down again)* Besides, we've found that it's best not to make friends with grown-ups, because…in the end…they don't act fair to you…But thank you; I'm very glad to have met you.

(She goes into the house. **FATHER** *takes off his cap and glasses;* **MOTHER** *her hat and veil. They place them on chairs.* **FATHER** *prepares to make a difficult golf stroke.)*

FATHER. Where *are* the children?

MOTHER. Oh, they're hiding somewhere, as usual.

FATHER. Hiding! Hiding from their father!

MOTHER. Or they're playing one of those awful games of theirs. Come in, come in. You'll see them at supper.

(She goes into the house.)

FATHER. *(He stands at the end of the stage farthest from the house and calls.)* Caroline! Dodie! Billee-ee-ee! *(Silence, of course. He goes into the house.)*

End of Play

YOUTH

This play became available through the research and editing of F. J. O'Neil of manuscripts in the Thornton Wilder Collection at Yale University.

CHARACTERS

LEMUEL GULLIVER, a shipwrecked sea captain, forty-six
MISTRESS BELINDA JENKINS, a commoner, eighteen
LADY SIBYL PONSONBY, a noble lady, twenty-four
THE DUKE OF CORNWALL, the island's governor, twenty-eight
SIMPSON, a commoner and builder, twenty
[**TWO BOY GUARDS**, fifteen]

SETTING

A tropical island.

(At the back, an opening through a thicket leads to the principal town. Forward on the stage is a palm-thatched summer house without walls. Under its roof is a rustic table and bench; on the table some worn books. On the floor at one side of the stage is a piece of glass, fringed with moss; this represents a spring.)

(GULLIVER, forty-six, drags himself on in the last stages of hunger and exhaustion. He sees the spring and avidly laps at it with hand and tongue. Somewhat refreshed, he lies down and closes his eyes. Then rising to a sitting position, he becomes aware of the summer house. He goes to it and opens one of the books. In great amazement he murmurs: "English! In English!")

(In the distance a young woman's voice is heard lilting a kind of yodel. It ceases and is resumed several times.)

(GULLIVER makes a shell of his hands and call:)

GULLIVER. Anyone?...Is anyone there?

BELINDA'S VOICE. What?...Wha...a...t?

GULLIVER. Is anyone there?

VOICE. *(nearer)* 'Oo are *you?*

GULLIVER. *(still calling)* I am an Englishman, madam, ship-wrecked on this island.

VOICE. 'Oo?...'Ooh?

GULLIVER. I am Captain Gulliver, at your service, madam.

VOICE. 'Ooh?

GULLIVER. Captain Gulliver – Lemuel Gulliver of the fourmaster *Arcturus*, Port of London, at your service, madam.

VOICE. Oh! Lord. 'Ow old are you? *(GULLIVER, nonplussed, does not answer.)* 'Ow *old* are you?

GULLIVER. I'm forty-six years of age.

VOICE. *(just offstage)* No!! No!! *Forty*-six! 'Ow did you get here?

GULLIVER. I was shipwrecked, madam. I have been in the sea for three days, pushing a spar. I am sorely in need of food and am much dependent on your kindness.

(Enter **MISTRESS BELINDA JENKINS,** *eighteen. She gazes at* **GULLIVER** *with growing abhorrence, covers her face with her hands and turns to the entrance through which she came.)*

BELINDA. Oh, Lady Sibyl! 'Ow 'ideous! 'Ow unbearable!

(Enter **LADY SIBYL PONSONBY,** *twenty-four. Both are charmingly dressed as of the eighteenth century in some textile-like tapa cloth.* **LADY SIBYL** *is a great lady, however, and carries a parasol tufted with seagulls' feathers)*

LADY SIBYL. *(staring at* **GULLIVER,** *but with more controlled repulsion; as though to herself.)* It's hall true! Then it's hall true, wot they say! *(pronounced "si")*

BELINDA. *(to* **GULLIVER,** *spitefully)* Turn your fice awigh! How can you look at Lady Sibyl?

LADY SIBYL. *(with authority)* 'Old your tongue, Jenkins.

BELINDA. *(pointing)* But he's terrible! He's terrible!

LADY SIBYL. *(coldly)* Yes. – You are 'ideous to behold.

GULLIVER. I'm a plain man, madam; and in addition I have been without food and drink for three days – and with very little sleep.

LADY SIBYL. *(again as though to herself)* I have never seen an old man before. *Forty*-six, you say? It's hall true, too true.

BELINDA. *(peeking from behind* **LADY SIBYL**) The wrinkles, your ladyship. Nobody could count them! – Can he see? Can he hear?

LADY SIBYL. *(from curiosity, not kindness)* You must be suffering in every part of your body?

GULLIVER. I have suffered, madam, principally from thirst until I found this spring here; and I would be most beholden to you if *you* could also graciously give me something to eat.

LADY SIBYL. I shall never forget this moment. You are, indeed, a most pitiable spectacle.

GULLIVER. *(with dignity)* I shall turn my face away if it distresses you, madam.

BELINDA. All of you is as repulsive as your face.

GULLIVER. I am as God made me and the hardships I have endured. – If you would graciously provide me with the means I could catch fish to [assuage] my hunger. I have been shipwrecked before and have sustained myself in many ways.

LADY SIBYL. *(musing)* At your age everything must be painful – exceedingly – breathing...and walking...

GULLIVER. *(loud)* Young woman, are you indeed deaf *(pronounced "deef")* or do you lack humanity? I am starving.

BELINDA. "Young woman!" You are talking to Lady Sibyl Ponsonby.

LADY SIBYL. Be quiet, Jenkins. – Old man, you will be given something to eat. There have been other old men on this island. They were given something to eat before they departed.

GULLIVER. I hope that will not be long.

LADY SIBYL. That will not be long.

GULLIVER. Did I understand you, madam, did I hear correctly: that you have never seen a man of forty-six before?

BELINDA. Forty-six! No one has ever seen anyone older than twenty-nine – except one that floated up from the sea, like yourself. There is no one on this island older than twenty-nine and there never will be.

GULLIVER. Merciful Heavens! What do you do with your older persons?

LADY SIBYL. I will now go and call someone to attend to your needs. You will not follow me! You will not leave this place. Today is a day of festival and it is of the highest importance that no one sees you – that is, as few as possible see you. – Jenkins, stay near him.

BELINDA. I, your ladyship!!

LADY SIBYL. Do not enter into conversation with him. *(appraising him coldly)* I do not think he could progress far.

BELINDA. *(becoming hysterical)* Oh, your ladyship, your lady-ship – do not leave me alone with him. I will become ill with the sight. *(She falls on her knees, clinging to* **LADY SIBYL.***)* I will become ill. I will become ill.

LADY SIBYL. Get up, Jenkins! – Very well, I will stay with this man. Go to the Duke of Cornwall. Draw him aside and speak to him in a low voice. Tell him that we have come upon this…foreigner. 'E will know what to do.

GULLIVER. *(gesturing as though bringing food to his mouth)* And tell him –

LADY SIBYL. Tell him the old man is hungry. – But, Jenkins, hold your tongue. Do not speak of it to anyone else.

BELINDA. To think that this should happen today – of all days! *(She sidles up toward* **GULLIVER** *and examines him intently. Softly.)* Think of all the years he has lived!

LADY SIBYL. Jenkins!

BELINDA. *(Still scanning* **GULLIVER***; half answering.)* Yes, milady.

LADY SIBYL. Jenkins! Do as I tell you!

BELINDA. Yes, milady; but I shall never see an old man again. I want to look at him… *(lower)* …he is not as abominable as he was at first. One gets used to him, a little. – Old man, have you wives…and children?

LADY SIBYL. Belinda! I shall have you jailed!

BELINDA. *(turning to her, with spirit)* Your ladyship, with all due respect to your ladyship, your ladyship has been extremely severe with me for many weeks. I care not if I go to jail. As I was the first person to see this old man I ask to be permitted to have a few words with him.

LADY SIBYL. Two minutes, Belinda…No more.

*(***LADY SIBYL*** turns her back on them and moves to the rear of the scene, striking her parasol on the floor.)*

GULLIVER. Yes, Mistress Jenkins, I have a wife Mary, a son John, and a daughter Betsy.

BELINDA. *(slowly, scarcely a question)* And are you very cruel to them?

GULLIVER. Madam?

BELINDA. *Old* men are cruel and nasty tempered. Everyone knows that.

*(**GULLIVER** gazes deep into her eyes with a faint smile, slowly shaking his head. She continues, as if to herself.)*

Your eyes are different from our eyes. Maybe some old men are a *little bit* kind.

*(**GULLIVER,** as though in friendly complicity, rubs his stomach with one hand and conveys the other to his mouth.)*

Yes, I will hurry. – I am going, your ladyship.

LADY SIBYL. And remember, no blabbing. *(She looks toward the sun, almost directly overhead.)* The games are about to begin. When you have delivered your message, take your place in silence.

BELINDA. *(curtsies)* Yes, your ladyship.

*(**BELINDA** goes out. **LADY SIBYL** starts strolling about with great self-possession.)*

GULLIVER. Surely, I did not hear correctly – *no* older men?

LADY SIBYL. I have no wish to enter into conversation with you.

GULLIVER. *(After a short pause, no longer able to contain himself.)* By God's body, madam, you cannot be of stone! You are not a child! I have not hitherto been regarded as a contemptible being. I have been received by kings and queens and have been their guest at meat...I am Captain Lemuel Gulliver. I am not a dog.

LADY SIBYL. I have never seen a dog, but I think you must greatly resemble one.

GULLIVER. Madam, you have seen nothing but one small island. You are not in a position to say that you have seen anything. I am astonished that you have no questions to put to me about the world that surrounds you.

LADY SIBYL. *(lofty smile)* What questions would those be, Captain Gullibo?

GULLIVER. Madam, ignorance is a misery, but there is one still greater: a lack of any desire to increase one's knowledge.

LADY SIBYL. But I have learned much from you in this short time. You have come from that world out there *(She indicates it lightly with her parasol; her voice turns suddenly vindictive.)* and you have brought its poisons with you. Your visible infirmities are also marks of the country from which you came. They must be as painful for you to bear as for us to behold. However, you will not have to bear them much longer.

*(**GULLIVER** gives up trying to understand her. He sinks down on the bench by the table. He is about to fall asleep.)*

Captain, it is not our custom for a commoner to be seated in the presence of the nobility.

*(**GULLIVER**, uncomprehending, raises his head)* I see; you are deaf. *(pronounced "deef")* I said: it is not the custom for a commoner to be seated in the presence of the nobility.

GULLIVER. *(dragging himself to his feet; with ironic deference)* Oh…oh…your ladyship will forgive me…my fatigue… and my hunger.

*(**LADY SIBYL** puts her hand into her reticule and brings out some lozenges, which she places on the table.)*

LADY SIBYL. While you are waiting, here are some comfits which I have been keeping…for my children.

GULLIVER. For your children, Lady Sibyl?

LADY SIBYL. Our children on this island live in a village of their own. They are well tended. They are happy. That is our custom here.

*(In astonishment, **GULLIVER** is about to ask a question. He corrects himself, and, bowing, says in a low voice.)*

GULLIVER. I thank your ladyship.

(He puts two into his mouth ravenously; then takes one out for decorum's sake. A musical sound, like a rolling chord from many harps, is heard from the city. **GULLIVER** *listens in astonishment.)*

May I ask your ladyship the source of that music?

LADY SIBYL. You forget everything you are told. Today is a day of great festival. *(she looks at the sun)* It is beginning with the children's Morris Dance and –

GULLIVER. Oh, milady, I would greatly wish to see this festival –

LADY SIBYL. *(slight laugh, "how unthinkable")* These will be followed by the Hoop Dance and the Dagger Dance. The Duke of Cornwall – who will be here in a moment – is the greatest victor in the Hoop Dance that has ever been known. He has won eight garlands. Moreover, he is the only man who has ever kept a kite in the air for an entire day.

GULLIVER. Ah!! He must indeed be remarkable!...An entire day!...I trust that the duke is of mature years?

LADY SIBYL. *(sharply)* I did not hear you correctly. (**GULLIVER** *does not repeat the question.)* He is naturally of mature years. He is our governor. He is twenty-eight *(pronounced "ite")*.

GULLIVER. *(stares at her; then with dawning horror)* Great Heavens, girl! What do you do with your older persons?

LADY SIBYL. Captain Gullibo, there is no profit in pursuing a conversation on matters you are not capable of understanding.

GULLIVER. *(shouting)* You kill them. You murder them when they reach the age of twenty-nine?

LADY SIBYL. How dare you address me in that manner? – Vulgar brutish Englander! Barbarian! How could you understand customs that are based on wisdom and reason.

GULLIVER. I dread to hear them! *(louder)* Are you able to answer me: what do you do to those who reach the age of twenty-nine?

LADY SIBYL. *(slowly; with serene assurance)* We drink the wine. We sleep. We are placed in a boat. The current carries us away.

GULLIVER. Thunder! This is hellish!

LADY SIBYL. *(putting a hand delicately on her ear)* Restrine your senile violence, Captain Gullibo.

GULLIVER. And *you*, your ladyship – are you going to drink that wine and go to sleep in that boat?

LADY SIBYL. When I am old – readily, gladly. I have four years to live. That is a very long time.

GULLIVER. And no one ever rebels? No one twenty-nine years old ever wishes to live longer?

LADY SIBYL. Captain Gullibo, you prate. You rive. You forget that you are old – very old. What I have told you is the custom of this island! Do you understand the word "custom"?…Would any of us *wish* to be…

GULLIVER. *(hand to head)* Your ladyship must permit me to sit down. *(he does)*

LADY SIBYL. *(strolling about and fanning herself)* It is understandable that the duke is occupied today. *(severely)* Your arrival is most inopportune.

GULLIVER. The matter was beyond my control, Lady Sibyl. Little did I know that I was arriving on this happy island on the great day of the Hoop Dance. On future occasions I shall arrange it with greater propriety.

LADY SIBYL. *(looks at him and raises her eyebrows)* Future occasions, Captain Gullibo? At your age, Captain, you cannot speak with certainty of future occasions.

GULLIVER. *(returning her glance; in a low voice)* Lady Sibyl, I am thinking of your children. You will never know the joys of seeing them grow into young manhood and womanhood. You will never hold grandchildren on your knees.

LADY SIBYL. You are tedious, Captain Gullibo. I have read of those things in books.

GULLIVER. Ah, madam. – You have books, I see.

LADY SIBYL. We have one hundred and twenty-seven books, Captain.

GULLIVER. *(lowers his head in admiration; after a pause, suddenly humble and earnest)* Lady Sibyl, let me throw myself upon your mercy. You are a woman, and women in all times have tempered this rough world with mercy and compassion. I have arrived a stranger and an interloper here; I do not wish to intrude upon this happy existence. I can see that you have much influence on this island; graciously exert it on my behalf. I saw that there were boats drawn up along the shore. I am a seaman of experience. When I have been given some food to stay my hunger, be my advocate with this Duke of Cornwall –

LADY SIBYL. *(purest amazement)* Where would you go?

GULLIVER. *(pointing)* ...That island or continent...those mountains...

LADY SIBYL. *(harshly)* I have nothing to do with such matters. Those fishing boats and their sails are fixed to the shore. They are locked with thongs that only a few nobles can undo. – You forget that you are old – very old. Your life is over. Anyone can see that.

(she turns away)

GULLIVER. I have a wife and children. – You said you have children?

LADY SIBYL. Naturally I have children.

GULLIVER. Look in your heart. Enable me to –

LADY SIBYL. Be silent!

GULLIVER. *(sinking onto the bench; to himself, in despair)* Yes... yes...Humanity is the last thing that will be learned by man. *(He puts his head on his arms and is about to fall asleep.)*

LADY SIBYL. *(walking up and down, loftily)* You may be certain that nothing will be done here that is not for the wisest and the best. We are enlightened here; and we are Christians. That strain of music you heard came from Westminster Abbey. The Archbishop of Canterbury is addressing the contestants in the games. If you were a *young* man we would be proud to show you how happy our existence is, and how perfect our institutions. This perfection is rendered possible by the fact that here we have no –

(GULLIVER has fallen asleep.)

GULLIVER. *(mumbling)* ...steep...the steep streets... Redriff, home!...Mary – Polly!...Polly, forgive me....

(He falls silent. LADY SIBYL gazes at him for a moment with repugnance, then draws nearer and scans his face intently – a long gaze. When he stirs and seems about to wake, she moves away and, opening her parasol, strolls off the stage.)

(In deep stupor GULLIVER slips off the bench and rolls under the table.)

(LADY SIBYL returns hurriedly; there is a suggestion of walking backward as though royalty were approaching. Enter the DUKE OF CORNWALL, twenty-eight, very splendid in festival dress. To the early eighteenth-century costume have been added feathers and colored shells, etc. He is followed by SIMPSON, twenty, a commoner, carrying a tray of food. The DUKE gazes fixedly at GULLIVER)

LADY SIBYL. He has fallen into a swound, your grace.

DUKE. Simpson – throw some water on his face.

(SIMPSON scoops some water from the mirror pool and throws it on GULLIVER's face. GULLIVER recovers consciousness, stirs and cumbrously extricates himself from under the table. Finally, he grasps the situation and, standing erect, confronts the DUKE, eye to eye.)

Who are you?

GULLIVER. Lemuel Gulliver, your grace, captain of the fourmaster *Arcturus*, Port of London.

DUKE. How old are you?

GULLIVER. I am in my middle years; I am forty-six.

DUKE. They tell me you have been three days without food – Simpson, place the food on the table. Eat!

GULLIVER. I thank your grace. Commoners do not sit in the presence of the nobility. I shall eat when you have left to take part in the festival. *(pause)* Sir, I have visited many countries and have been shipwrecked on the shores of several. In all of them, save one, I have been treated with courtesy as a citizen of England and a subject of our gracious sovereign, Queen Anne. I am indebted to you for this relief from my hunger. I trust that hereafter I may see your cities and learn of your customs. In return I shall gladly tell you of other parts of the world that I have visited; and above all of the country whose language you speak and from which your ancestors came.

DUKE. *(again a short contemptuous pause; then with a curt gesture of the hand)* You are tedious, old man. – Simpson!

SIMPSON. Yes, your grace?

DUKE. Withdraw to a distance. It is not suitable that a commoner hear this nonsense. I shall call you when it is time for you to stand watch over the captain.

*(***SIMPSON*** bows and goes out. ***GULLIVER*** begins to laugh to himself and, turning away, sits down.)*

LADY SIBYL. *(revolted)* He is laughing!!

GULLIVER. To be young, and yet ask no questions about the country from which your ancestors came! To be young, and yet have no curiosity concerning the shore that lies upon the horizon! To be young, and yet – oh, ye immortal Gods! – to be without adventure of mind or generosity of spirit! Now it is clear to me why you so gladly bring your lives to a close at the age of twenty-nine – *gladly* was Lady Sibyl's word.

DUKE. *(bitingly)* That should not be difficult for you to understand – you, with this decay of mind and body –

GULLIVER. *(interrupting)* No! No, it is not the advance of age that frightens you on this island. *(with a sardonic smile)* A greater enemy threatens you. *(abruptly changing the subject)* I do not wish to detain your grace from the festival and from your trophies.

DUKE. Come, Lady Sibyl.

GULLIVER. Permit me, however, one question.

(the **DUKE** nods)

What is the name of this island and this country?

DUKE. Name? Why should it have a name?

GULLIVER. I have visited twenty countries. Each has borne a name in which it takes pride.

DUKE. Proud? All of them were proud?

GULLIVER. They were. They are.

DUKE. Among those twenty countries was there one that was not governed by old men – governed, misgoverned, burdened, oppressed by old men? By the pride and avarice, and the lust for power of old men? One which did not constantly war at the instigation of old men like *yourself*, to enlarge its boundaries; to enslave others; to enrich itself? We know of the War of the Roses. Or by the religious bigotry of old men – we know of the Saint Bartholomew Massacre, [the] murder of Charles, king and martyr. And when these prides of yours have obtained their lands, whose bodies are those lying upon the field of battle? – They are the bodies of men under thirty. We need no name to distinguish this country from others. Say that you are in the Country of the Young.

GULLIVER. So be it! – Since you do not wish me to encumber you longer, I request some boat with which I may rid you of my presence. *(in amazement)* How did you come here? Who brought you here?

DUKE. God!

GULLIVER. God! – Where did you acquire this distrust and hatred of the old?

DUKE. We have no boats for that purpose.

GULLIVER. The smallest would serve me.

DUKE. No boat of ours has ever made that journey and never will.

GULLIVER. Perhaps your grace will let me purchase a boat. This ring was given to me by the King of Laputa. It is of pure alchemist's gold.

DUKE. You have been here a few hours. Lady Sibyl has told me that already you have offered us insult and have spoken of our customs with contempt; and now you wish to introduce barter and trafficking, and gold! – gold, which is above all the instrument by which old men keep the younger in subjection. There is no gold and no trading here. You shall never leave this island and you shall not long envenom it. We shall make you a present for which we ask no return. We shall give you the only happiness that still lies open to you.

GULLIVER. Duke of Cornwall – Duke of Palm Trees and Sand! I wish you a happy twenty-ninth birthday. I can understand that you will gladly drink the wine and welcome the long sleep. Twenty-nine years of jumping through hoops and flying kites will have been enough. Already you are advancing toward a decay worse than age – yes, toward boredom, infinite boredom. Youth left to itself is a cork upon the waves. As we say of the young: they do not know what to do with themselves. It is only under the severity – the well-wishing severity – of your elders that you can shake from yourselves the misery of your aimless state. You elect yourselves into societies and call yourselves dukes and earls; did I hear correctly that each man on this island has several wives? You play games. What more can you ask of a thirtieth birthday than a deep slumber!

LADY SIBYL. *(ablate)* Your grace! How can you let him speak to you so?!

DUKE. *(with a smile)* But this is what we knew; foul and embittered age! Envy and jealousy! Despising those things of which he is no longer capable. *(whimsically to* **LADY SIBYL***)* Perhaps we should take this man and exhibit him for all to see.

LADY SIBYL. *(covering her face)* Your grace!

GULLIVER. Yes, and for all to hear, your grace.

DUKE. And to hear. – What would you say to them?

GULLIVER. Why, I should tell them that if a man is not civilized between the ages of twelve and twenty – civilized by his elders – he will never be civilized at all. *(*LADY SIBYL *covers her ears.)* And oh, it is not an easy task. To educate young men is like rolling boulders up to the tops of mountains; the whole community is engaged in the work and with what doubtful success! For every *one* Isaac Newton or Christopher Wren there are thousands who roll to the bottom of the mountain and occupy themselves with jumping through hoops. *(He sways from weakness, his hand to his head and heart.)* Go to your dances and garlands. I can see that your happiness has begun to stale already. You are weary of life. Old age has marked you already.

DUKE. *(with supreme complaisance)* Oh, I'm young enough! *(he calls)* Mr. Simpson! Mr. Simpson!!

(The sound of music has been rising from the distance. Enter SIMPSON.*)*

SIMPSON. Yes, your grace?

DUKE. Simpson, you are in charge of this man. See that he does not leave this clearing. Do not enter into conversation with him. It would suffocate you. Later I shall send someone to replace you – Lady Sibyl!

*(*LADY SIBYL*'s hand has gone to her forehead; her parasol and reticule fall. She is about to faint.)*

LADY SIBYL. Oh, your grace…this sight…has sickened me.

DUKE. *(cold fury)* Take command of yourself!

(With a gesture he orders SIMPSON *to pick up the fallen objects.* SIMPSON *does so and holds them ready for* LADY SIBYL*)*

LADY SIBYL. *(swaying; with closed eyes)* I must breathe a moment.

DUKE. Fool! *(he strikes her sharply on both cheeks)* Go to the city!

GULLIVER. *(taking two steps forward)* You strike her!! You strike her!

DUKE. We permit no weakness here – neither ours nor yours.

GULLIVER. *(turns and seats himself on the bench by the table)* Humanity is the last thing that will be learned by man; it will not be learned from the young.

*(**LADY SIBYL** has taken her parasol and reticule. She collects her dignity, but is scarcely able to leave the stage.)*

DUKE. Simpson!

SIMPSON. Your grice!

DUKE. If you fail at any point in your guard over this man, you will be put to the press – and you know what press I mean. And you will be removed from your office as builder and constructor. *(He looks appraisingly at **GULLIVER**.)* If he tries to leave the clearing, kick him strongly at the shinbones.

*(He goes out. **SIMPSON** takes his stand at a distance from **GULLIVER** whom he watches intently. **GULLIVER** returns to his meal, but seems to have lost his appetite. Again there is a sound of music from the city. **GULLIVER** rises and listens.)*

GULLIVER. Is there no way, Mr. Simpson, that I may view the games from a distance?

*(**SIMPSON** shakes his head.)*

I am sorry. *(He eats a little.)* They must be a wonderful sight...wonderful. Hoops and kites. *(pause)* You strike women...is that often, Mr. Simpson?...Do you strike women frequently, Mr. Simpson? *(no reply)* ...You are very proud of your civilization...when you are angry you *strike* and you *torture...* *(**SIMPSON** mutters something)* I did not hear what you said, Mr. Simpson.

SIMPSON. He is old. Strikes and tortures because 'e is old. 'E will die next year.

GULLIVER. He will be killed next year. That is not quite the same thing as merely dying. He will be killed. No wonder he is excitable, Mr. Simpson. In the normal way of life we grow of a more mild and kindly disposition with the years. *(he eats)* So you are a builder and constructor, Mr. Simpson. You are an architect. Lady Sibyl spoke of a Westminster Abbey. I would like to see it. Did you build this Westminster Abbey, sir? *(no answer)* You have great storms in this part of the world – far greater than London has. You must build very – solidly. Have you rock here?

*(**SIMPSON** points off. **GULLIVER** rises and peers in the direction.)*

Coral limestone, I presume. Not easy. Arches and a vaulted roof. Ah, you should see the dome of St. Paul's. There's a sight, Mr. Simpson… *(he eats)* I am glad that you feel no disposition to talk, sir. I was afraid that you might ask me questions about the life led by young men like yourself in my country. *(pause)* It would fill me with shame to describe it to you. *(He lowers his voice as though imparting a discreditable secret.)* Imagine it! You would be working all the time to acquire more knowledge: from morning to night – and at night by lamplight. Think: to be a better doctor, to govern the people more wisely, *to be a better builder*, Mr. Simpson. Go down on your knees, sir, and thank your Maker that you live on this happy island where learning never penetrates, where young men are not encouraged by old men to extend their knowledge and their skill.

SIMPSON. *(loudly)* The old men drive them like slaves; the old men take the credit and the profit.

GULLIVER. The young men succeed them. They are not killed at twenty-nine. They become master builders themselves and may decide whether they will be just or unjust. However, I do not wish to talk about it. I reproach myself that I am preventing you from taking part in the games.

SIMPSON. Commoners do not take part in the games.

GULLIVER. Ah! *(he eats)*

*(**SIMPSON** gazes at him, brooding)*

SIMPSON. I'm a builder.

GULLIVER. *(looking up at the summerhouse)* Ah! – you made *this?*

SIMPSON. Aye – and the new Westminster Abbey.

GULLIVER. Westminster Abbey! Then you are the chief builder.

SIMPSON. The chief builder is an earl. He has no time to build.

GULLIVER. The new Abbey is of stone – of sandstone or coral?

SIMPSON. The pillars at the corners are.

GULLIVER. And the roof?

(**SIMPSON** *shakes his head.* **GULLIVER** *points to the thatch.*)

Of thatch? – of palm boughs?

(**SIMPSON** *nods*)

But, man, you have severe storms here. Ah! *(he looks up)* Mr. Simpson, the storm that cast me on your shores has damaged this charming…shelter, this pagoda. Was your Westminster Abbey able to sustain the fury of that wind and rain?

(**SIMPSON** *stares straight before him.*)

You will not answer me, man! Your Abbey seats – what? – four hundred. Of what is your roof? Of palm fronds? (**SIMPSON**, *without moving his eyes, nods.*)

I see! When storm destroys your Westminster Abbey you build another. I see! I see! You don't know how to make an arch or a buttress. Oh, Mr. Simpson, do not ask me the secrets of the arch, the buttress and the dome. You are happy. Remain happy. Do not let us think of all the labor that went into those discoveries.

SIMPSON. *(taking steps toward* **GULLIVER***; in a low voice)* Sir… Mr. Captain… *(His hands describe an arch.)* Do you know how to pile stone…so they will not fall?

GULLIVER. Believe me. Mr. Simpson, I did not arrive in this paradise in order to poison it with thoughts of progress and industry.

SIMPSON. But you *do* know?

GULLIVER. Perhaps in a hundred years some unhappy youth will be born with talent – with genius. *He* will light upon the laws of the arch. He will prove that youth stands in no need of its elders, no need of the accumulated wisdom of its ancestors. *He will make a roof*...Bring your ear nearer, young man the dome of St. Paul's... *(His hand descries a high dome.)*

SIMPSON. How high is it?

GULLIVER. How high? Sixty men standing on one another's shoulders could not touch the top of it.

SIMPSON. *(back three yards)* You are lying! All old men lie. Eat your food. Go to sleep. I ask you a question and you give me a lie.

*(**SIMPSON** has raised his head.)*

GULLIVER. What I said is true, but your rebuke is justified. There is no greater unkindness than to arouse ambition in a young man. – But *you* are to blame. You asked me a question. *(with assumed indignation)* A few more questions like that and you'll be proposing that we take a *boat* and cross to that shore. No I'll not go, I tell you.

SIMPSON. *(sullenly)* The boats are tied and we cannot untie them.

GULLIVER. Yes, those thongs the nobles keep... *(His eyes are looking off speculatively.)*

SIMPSON. They're twisted and untwisted with hooks of iron.

GULLIVER. Iron?

SIMPSON. Aye, they're the only pieces of metal on the island. The nobles keep them.

GULLIVER. Very wise! Some fool might think of journeying out there...for knowledge and science. – Understand, young man, I'll not leave this island. Give me this day here; then bring the wine and the long sleep. Why should a man trouble his head raising domes? Fly kites, jump through hoops, beget children and sleep.

SIMPSON. *(after a pause, grumbling unintelligibly)* These things you call secrets...

GULLIVER. I cannot understand you, sir.

SIMPSON. These things you call the secrets of the arch and the...batless – old men keep these secrets to themselves, that's certain.

GULLIVER. *(sternly)* Cease, Mr. Simpson, to talk of things you know nothing about.

SIMPSON. How would a young man learn them?

GULLIVER. You are asking dangerous questions, Mr. Simpson. – Let me bid you again to go down on your knees and thank your Maker that you do not live in a country where older men would urge you and struggle with you and encourage you to enrich yourself with all learning and skill.

SIMPSON. I don't believe you.

GULLIVER. – A young man would learn them by crossing that water and finding his way into a world that does not spend all its time in games and dances.

SIMPSON. *(mumbles)* I do not believe you. *(suddenly loud)* All old men are wicked.

GULLIVER. *(simply)* I am the only old man you have ever seen.

SIMPSON. *(approaching* **GULLIVER**, *the beginning of violence)* Then tell me –

GULLIVER. What?

SIMPSON. The secrets: the arch and the batless.

GULLIVER. *(backing away)* I do not know them.

SIMPSON. *(seizing* **GULLIVER**'*s throat)* Tell me them! Wicked old man, tell me them!

GULLIVER. *(forced to his knees)* I am not a builder. I am a doctor and a seaman.

SIMPSON. *(as they struggle)* I will not let you go before you tell me –

*(***GULLIVER*** faints. Pause. ***SIMPSON*** leans over him and calls:)*

Old man! Old man!

*(Enter **BELINDA** carrying a tray and more fruit. She starts back in consternation)*

BELINDA. *(whispering)* Is he dead?...Have *you* killed him?

SIMPSON. *(sullenly)* No...he has died of his old age.

*(**BELINDA** puts her ear to **GULLIVER**'s mouth)*

BELINDA. I think he is still breathing. It is a swound. *(Both are on their knees gazing at **GULLIVER**.)* Now I do not think he is ugly at all. I think he is a friend.

SIMPSON. *(moves away in inner turmoil)* I do not understand a word he says. He should not have come here.

BELINDA. *(as before)* What a strange thing wrinkles are. *(Unconsciously she strokes her face...softly.)* I could ask him questions all day. – Mr. Simpson, let him go back to his own people.

SIMPSON. *(harshly)* How could he do that?

*(**BELINDA** slowly draws from her apron pocket a hook of iron. **SIMPSON** draws back in horror.)*

BELINDA. *(lowering her voice)* This is the hook that was lost last year. It was on Lady Sibyl's dressing table. I think she put it there for me to find it. I think she has hidden it to spite the Duke of Cornwall. *(She holds it out toward **SIMPSON**.)* Unlock the boat and let the man go.

SIMPSON. No!

BELINDA. *(Gazes at **GULLIVER**. Pause. Low, with energy.)* Go with him!...He is not strong enough to sail the boat alone. Go.

SIMPSON. Do not speak to me! No, I will not go...among other men...I do not know anything. *He* does not know that we commoners cannot read. Every – *over there* – would see that I am a booby.

BELINDA. Mr. Simpson! Look at him. Come close and look at him! He would be your friend...I think *some* old people are good.

SIMPSON. No, I will not go.

BELINDA. He is waking up. Go away and think; but take the hook.

(**SIMPSON** *takes the hook and goes off.*)

GULLIVER. *(Opens his eyes. Pause. Sees **BELINDA**.)* Oh! You are here...Where is the young man?

BELINDA. He is nearby...will you tell me your name again?

GULLIVER. Captain Gulliver.

BELINDA. Captain Gulliver. If you came to your home again what would you do first?

GULLIVER. Mistress Jenkins, I would go up the steep street – you have never seen a steep street! – I think it would be at sunset...I would knock at the door...My wife or one of my children would come to the door... *(pause)* ...Soon we would sit down at the table, and give thanks to God...and eat...

BELINDA. *(laughing, scandalized)* Captain Gulliver, you would sit down with your wife!!

GULLIVER. Do not husband and wives –

BELINDA. No – !! *(she laughs)* Sit down! No man has ever eaten with a woman – ! The men eat all by themselves. The nobles in one place. The commoners in another. And the boys when they are six by themselves.

GULLIVER. And if I lived on this happy island, when would I see my daughter? *(She does not answer.)* You remember your father?

BELINDA. Yes.

GULLIVER. You saw him often? You loved him?

BELINDA. But...men live...*over there...*

GULLIVER. The childhood of the race...You have slipped five-ten thousand years...

(**SIMPSON** *has returned, and half hidden, is listening.*)

In a thousand years, Mistress Jenkins, gradually on this island things will change. A man will have one wife and only one wife. I think when your father died at twenty-nine he was just beginning to understand (**GULLIVER** *points to his forehead*) what the joys of being your father could be – but it was too late.

(**GULLIVER** *clasps* **BELINDA** *by her shoulders, sadly*)

GULLIVER. *(cont.)* You all die here just before a new world of mind and heart is open to you.

[*(The music and sounds of celebration have increased, as if approaching.* **SIMPSON** *breaks from his hiding place and rushes to* **GULLIVER** *with the iron hook.* **SIMPSON** *pulls at* **GULLIVER**'s *arm and points toward the sea.* **GULLIVER** *grasps the situation immediately, starts to go with* **SIMPSON**, *but looks back at* **BELINDA**. *She remains motionless, staring straight ahead, and does not meet his glance.* **SIMPSON** *drags* **GULLIVER** *off.)*

(Music is louder. **BELINDA** *gazes front; intense, conflicted. Pause.)*

(**SIMPSON** *reappears running. He takes both of* **BELINDA**'s *hands in his. They look at each other. A decision passes between them.* **BELINDA** *casts one glance back over her shoulder at all she has ever known; and they run off to join* **GULLIVER**.*)*

(Music increases.)

(Two **BOY GUARDS**, *fifteen, rush in with ropes to bind* **GULLIVER** *for his ceremonial death. The* **DUKE** *enters behind. They look about, see that* **GULLIVER**, **SIMPSON** *and* **BELINDA** *are gone. The* **DUKE** *is the first to realize the implication of this absence. He stands upstage center as the* **GUARDS** *roughly search everywhere. Convinced that the man they were after has escaped, they turn to the* **DUKE**.*)*

(Music takes on a wild, threatening sound.)

(The **DUKE** *has been gazing out toward a horizon, perhaps seeing the boat moving off, perhaps contemplating his own soon wasted mortality. The* **BOY GUARDS** *gaze intently at him as the lights fade)*]

End of Play

A NOTE ON THE TEXT

The author's manuscript existed in a partial typescript, which contained Wilder's handwritten corrections interleaved with several handwritten pages of clearly indicated revised material. The author's manuscript ended with Gulliver's speech to Belinda, spoken while Simpson listens hidden from their view. To conclude the play for production, I felt it would be helpful to take into account Wilder's most plausible intention: that Swift's Gulliver, only borrowed for this adventure, be returned safely to London and his place in English literature.

What then of Simpson and Belinda? Belinda had earlier insisted to Simpson that Gulliver was not strong enough to make the trip alone. Her plea that Simpson accompany Gulliver in the escape strongly suggests that Wilder intended Simpson and Gulliver to leave the island together. Simpson had been sent off with the tool that unlocks the boats. Further, there is the duke's threat that Simpson will be put to the press if he fails in his guard duties. Will Belinda stay behind to face the wrath of the Duke? Gulliver has developed a strong paternal feeling for her and, in addition, she and Simpson are commoners, both of age, both bright and interested and curious by nature: a matched set to be saved on Gulliver's "ark."

And the Duke? Wilder often placed characters in a position where, experiencing an epiphany, they catch a glimpse of what lies ahead. *Youth* seems constructed for just such a moment. The twenty-eight-year-old duke, himself within a year of his enforced demise, returns as he must, accompanied by his callow bullyish guards. Might Wilder perhaps have wanted us to wonder what the Duke feels about the defeat of his will and authority in the light of what he will not be able to avoid in a year's time? Those questions hang in the added final tableau.

F. J. O'Neil
April 1997

THE RIVERS UNDER THE EARTH
(Middle Age?)

This play became available through the research and editing of F. J. O'Neil of manuscripts in the Thornton Wilder Collection at Yale University.

CHARACTERS

MRS. CARTER, mother, thirty-eight
TOM, her son, sixteen
FRANCESCA, her daughter, seventeen
MR. CARTER, their father, forty-three

SETTING

A few years ago. A point of land near a lake in southern Wisconsin.

(At both sides of the stage are boxes of various sites, but none very large – orange boxes, canned goods boxes, covered with burlap or bits of rug. These are rocks. The action of this play takes place in the dark, but I wish it to be played in bright light. **MRS. CARTER**, *very attractive and looking less than her thirty-eight years, enters tentatively feeling her way in the dark. She is followed by her son,* **TOM**, *sixteen.)*

MRS. CARTER. Take my hand, Tom. I don't know where you children inherited your ability to see in the dark.

*(***TOM*** passes her and starts slowly leading her forward.)*

TOM. It isn't dark at all. All these stars reflected in the lake. – There's a sort of path here, Mother. The rocks are at the side of it.

MRS. CARTER. *(stopping)* Fireflies. All those fireflies. *(pause)* I don't know why it is that when I see fireflies I think of *horses* – no, of an old horse named Billy that we used to have when we were children.

TOM. Fireflies – and a horse!!

MRS. CARTER. *(still standing and smiling)* There are many associations like that one can't explain. – Why does your father dislike the color green? Why do I always make a mistake when I add a six and a seven? Why have I an ever so faint tiny prejudice against people whose name begins with B-Blodgetts and Burnses and Binghams and even dear old Mrs. Becket.

*(***TOM*** leads her a step forward.)*

TOM. I haven't got any quirks like that.

MRS. CARTER. *(stopping again)* Why have we never been able to make you eat rice?

TOM. Ugh! – I just don't like it!

MRS. CARTER. Why does your sister hate to sit in the back-seat of automobiles?

TOM. Oh, Francesca's crazy, anyway.

MRS. CARTER. Oh, no she isn't. She's the most reasonable and logical of us all.

TOM. Why does Francesca hate to come here?

MRS. CARTER. What?

TOM. She hates to come out on this point of land. She told me once – but then she was sorry she told me. She told me that every now and then she dreamed that she was on this point of land, and that when she dreamed it, it was a nightmare and she woke up crying or screaming or something.

MRS. CARTER. *(thoughtful)* You mustn't tease her about it. Promise me you won't tease her about it.

TOM. All right.

MRS. CARTER. Now take my elbow and lead me to a rock that I can remember at the very tip of the point. *(as they progress)* No – all those quirks, as you call them, are like wrecks at the bottom of the sea. They mark the place where there was once a naval battle – or a storm. Why did my dear father always become angry whenever anybody mentioned… – Thank you, Tom. Here it is! I used to come and sit here when I was a girl. There aren't any snakes are there?

TOM. *(competent)* One: snakes don't like this kind of pine needles; two: snakes in America don't come out at night.

MRS. CARTER. You're such a pleasure, Tom; you know everything. What I mean is: you know everything comforting. – Now you go back and do whatever it is you were doing.

*(**TOM** stands irresolute in the middle of the stage, looking up.)*

TOM. When do you want me to come and lead you back?

MRS. CARTER. Forget me, Tom. I can find my way back now.

(Girl's voice off: "T-o-o-m!...Tom C-a-a-arter.")

TOM. *(warningly, to his mother)* Hsh!

(The voice, passing in the distance: "T-o-o-m!")

TOM. Polly Springer's always wanting something. Golly, those girls are helpless. They can't even stick a marshmallow on a fork...The moon will rise over *there*...You came to this very place?

MRS. CARTER. In those days we knew everyone in all the houses around the lake. Many times I'd come and spend the night with the Wilsons...or the Kimballs. *(She indicates first the right, then the left.)* And I'd slip away from them, and come here; and think...We were told that this point had been some sort of Indian ceremonial campground...and a burial place, I suppose. Your father used to find arrowheads here.

TOM. What did you used to think about?

MRS. CARTER. Oh, what do young girls think about?...I remember once...I made a vow: never to marry. Yes. I was going to be a doctor. And at the same time I was going to be a singer. But I wasn't going to sing in concerts...for money. I was going to sing to my patients in the wards just before they turned out the lights for the night. That's the kind of thing young girls think about.

*(*TOM *has been taking this in very gravely, his eyes on the distance. He says abruptly.)*

TOM. But you *did* get married. And you almost never sing anymore. – I brought your guitar.

MRS. CARTER. What!?

TOM. Yes. I knew they'd ask you to sing later – around the bonfire.

MRS. CARTER. Why, Tom, you little devil. They would never have thought of it. Now don't you go putting the idea into their heads.

TOM. I didn't. I heard them talking about it. I canoed back across the lake and got your guitar...You don't *hate* to sing.

MRS. CARTER. Oh, I'll sing, if anybody asks me to. It's not important enough to make any discussion about.

(Silence. **TOM** *lies down in the path facing the sky, his head on his folded arms.)*

TOM. Right up there…in the Milky Way…There's something called a Coal Hole.

MRS. CARTER. What?

TOM. A Coal Hole. It's sort of a deep empty stocking. If Father gave me a Jaguar; and I started driving five thousand miles a minute – *starting* from up there – it'd take me hundreds of millions of years to get halfway through it. – Lake water has a completely different sound of slapping – or lapping – than water at the seashore, hasn't it? I like it best.

(He shuts his eyes. Girls' voices, giggling and talking excitedly, are heard near the entrance. **TOM** *sits up energetically and calls:)*

TOM. Mildred! Constance! – Is that you, Constance?

VOICE. Ye-e-s!

TOM. Get me a hamburger! Be a sweetie!

VOICE. *(sweetly)* Get it yourself, deeeer bo-oo-y.

TOM. *(lying down again; darkly)* The slaves are getting uppish at the end of the summer.

MRS. CARTER. Would these be the same trees that were here twenty years ago?

TOM. Yes. Red pines grow fast the first five years, then they settle down and grow about a foot a year. *(He turns to lie on his stomach, leaning on his elbow. He explains simply and casually.)* This is really a sand dune here. Until recently there was a great big lake over all this area. When the lake shrunk, there were these dunes. Ordinarily, it takes about five thousand years for the first grasses to get their roots in and to make enough humus for small bushes to grow. Then it takes about 10,000 years for the bushes to make enough humus for the white pines. Then come the red pines. Probably it was faster here because of these rocks. They prevented the top sand from being blown away every few days. That's why the trees are so much bigger here, and over at the Cavanaughs, and around the boat club...Rocks.

FRANCESCA'S VOICE. *(off)* Mo-o-ther!

MRS. CARTER. Yes, dear, here I am.

(Enter **FRANCESCA,** *seventeen, with a scarf.)*

FRANCESCA. Father said you'd probably be here.

TOM. *(rolling to one side)* Don't step on me, you galoot!

FRANCESCA. Oh, you're here. – Goodness, a regular jungle. – Father said you're to put this shawl on. He's bringing a blanket.

MRS. CARTER. I'm too warm as it is. Well, give it to me. Thank you, dear.

FRANCESCA. What are you doing out here?

TOM. *(bitingly)* We're talking about you. *(imitating a teacher)* "I was just saying to Mrs. Carter I don't know what's to become of Francesca. In all my ninety years of teaching I've never known such a problem child."

FRANCESCA. *(airily; leaving)* Tz-tz-tz.

TOM. *(urgently)* Be a sweet little flower box and get me a hamburger.

FRANCESCA. Mother, don't you let Tom have another. Everybody's laughing at him. James Wilson says he had eight. – If you want to make a howling pig of yourself, you can just get up and fetch your own. *(leaning over him maliciously)* Of course, I don't know what Miss What's-Her-Name will think of you gorging yourself like that. – Mother, Tom has been making a perfect fool of himself over a new girl – a cousin of the Richardsons. Anybody can see she's a perfect nothing, but there's Tom: "Violet, you didn't get any peach ice cream. Violet..."

TOM. *(covering her speech)* Quack-quack-quack. Honk-honk-honk.

FRANCESCA. Violet this and Violet that. *(louder)* He even started a fight over her.

TOM. *(rising and starting off)* Quack-quack-quack! I'll be back. Honk-honk-honk.

*(*TOM *leaves.)*

MRS. CARTER. When you're by yourself, Francesca, you're of course much older than Tom. But when you're *with* Tom, you're younger – and *much* younger. I wish someone could explain that to me.

FRANCESCA. Well, as far as I'm concerned, he's been an eight-year-old for years. And always will be.

MRS. CARTER. To get to know the best of Tom, you must learn to *(She puts her hand on her lips.)* hold your tongue. It's always a pleasure to be silent with Tom. You try it someday.

FRANCESCA. Why should I hold my tongue with him?

MRS. CARTER. Have you noticed how your father holds his tongue with you?

FRANCESCA. I don't talk *all the time* when I'm with Father.

MRS. CARTER. No. But when you do, you talk so *well.*

FRANCESCA. *(softened; with wonder)* Do I? *(kneeling before her mother)* Do I, really?

MRS. CARTER. I shouldn't have to tell you that.

FRANCESCA. Thank you.

*(enter **MR. CARTER**, forty-three, lawyer, with a blanket)*

MR. CARTER. Mary?

MRS. CARTER. Here I am, Fred.

MR. CARTER. Try this rock. It's drier. *(He puts the blanket on a rock.)* Can you see?

MRS. CARTER. *(crossing)* Yes. – What's this about a fight Tom had?

FRANCESCA. He's in a terrible mood tonight. First, that fight with the MacDougal boy – I wasn't there. Just some craziness or other.

MRS. CARTER. Do you know anything about it, Fred?

MR. CARTER. Yes. I'll tell you about it later.

FRANCESCA. But that's not really what upset him. A very funny thing happened. Before supper we were all lying around the dock and somebody said that you were going to sing tonight at the bonfire. And that boy from Milwaukee said: "Mrs. Carter sing! *She's too old!*" (**FRANCESCA** *thinks this is very funny. Gales of laughter*) He'd mixed you up with Mrs. Cavanaugh!! And Paul or Herb said: "She isn't *old.* She isn't any older than…" their own mothers. And the boy from Milwaukee said: "Sure, she's old. She's nice and all that, but she oughtn't to be allowed to sing." He thought Mrs. Cavanaugh was *you*!! (*more laughter*) But you should have seen Tom's face!

MRS. CARTER. What?

FRANCESCA. Tom's face. You'd have thought he was seeing a ghost. And the boy from Milwaukee said: "Why, she's got all those gray hairs." (*gales of laughter*) You remember how at breakfast a few days ago you said you'd found some more gray hairs?

MRS. CARTER. Yes.

FRANCESCA. And Tom was *believing* all this was about you. Well, I thought he'd either…jump on the boy and kill him, or go away and…maybe throw up.

MR. CARTER. What did he do?

MRS. CARTER. He canoed back across the lake to get my guitar.

MR. CARTER. Francesca, I want to talk to your mother alone a moment.

FRANCESCA. (*touch of pique*) All right…but kindly don't… mention…*me.*

(*She goes out; very queenly. Pause.*)

MR. CARTER. Well, what do you think about that?…I suppose in the code, a boy can't strike another boy for calling his mother an old woman…Tom learns about old age.

MRS. CARTER. What was this other story about a fight?

MR. CARTER. Very odd. Very odd. Tom is not a bulldog type. There's a new girl here – a cousin of the Richardsons. I don't know her name.

MRS. CARTER. Violet.

MR. CARTER. Yes, Violet Richardson. It looks as though Tom had taken a sudden fancy to her. She doesn't seem interesting to me – neither pretty nor individual. Anyway, he was sitting beside her – and the MacDougal boy – the bigger one – Ben – came up and began pulling at her arm...to get her to go over where some of them were dancing. Suddenly Tom got up in an awful rage. Told him to let her alone. She was talking to him. Not to stick his nose in where he wasn't wanted. It all flared up in a second: two furious roosters; two stags fighting over a doe. The MacDougal boy backed down. I think he went home. It was all over in a second, too – but it was *real*...it was very real and hot.

(slight pause)

MRS. CARTER. And I thought this was going to be just one more dull picnic!

(**MR. CARTER** *lights a pipe and goes to sit on the rock where his wife had been sitting.*)

Fred, Tom just told me that Francesca hated to come *here* – that she had bad dreams about it? Did you ever know that?

MR. CARTER. What? – Here, this point of land!

MRS. CARTER. Can you think of any reason for it?

MR. CARTER. No!

MRS. CARTER. I'll give you a hint: a robin redbreast.

MR. CARTER. What are you getting at?

MRS. CARTER. A dead robin?...The children were about six and seven. We had told them there had been an Indian graveyard here. They had found a dead robin in the woods, and they set out to bury it...I came on such solemn hymn singing and preaching and praying... That night Francesca was deathly ill –

MR. CARTER. Do I remember!! It was one of the most shattering experiences in my life!!

MRS. CARTER. Dr. Macintosh kept asking us what she had eaten, and I – stupidly, stupidly – failed to connect convulsions and hysterics with the burial of Robin Red Breast. Francesca had learned about death…You sat soothing her and reading aloud to her until the sun rose.

MR. CARTER. And ever since she dislikes the color red.

MRS. CARTER. And the same experience had no effect on Tom, whatever. Yet we always think of Tom as the sensitive one and Francesca as the sensible one.

MR. CARTER. I guess, growing up is one long walk among perils – among yawning abysses… *(silence)* Well, since you're talking about old times – I'm going to interrogate you. We've just heard that Tom had a fight. A fight over a girl named Violet. Does the name Violet bring back anything to you?

MRS. CARTER. No…No, why?

MR. CARTER. The color?

MRS. CARTER. No.

MR. CARTER. Think a minute. *(she shakes her head)* A dress you wore?

MRS. CARTER. Fred, you wouldn't remember that! Your sister brought me back from Italy that beautiful silk. I had a dress made from it.

MR. CARTER. Go on.

MRS. CARTER. Then I bought various things to match it… beads…

MR. CARTER. I called it "your violet year"…perfume!…

MRS. CARTER. Absurd…just before the war…1940 and '41. *(pause)* What are you implying? Tom wouldn't have known anything about that!

MR. CARTER. *(dismissing it unhesitatingly)* Of course not. He would have been only two. *(with teasing, flirtatious intention)* It was *myself* I was thinking of. He is infatuated with a Violet, just as I was.

MRS. CARTER. Now, go away…to think wives wear…you're in the way, Fred.

MR. CARTER. *(with a low laugh)* Well, I've had my troubles on that rock, too.

(TOM appears at the entrance, carrying a guitar.)

TOM. I could have found my way here by the smell of Father's pipe. *(He stops, closes his eyes and smells it.)* Christmas is coming. You'll need some more of that tobacco. *(he gropes)* I know its name. No, don't help me…ah! "Bonny Prince Charlie."

(He puts the guitar on his mother's lap)

MRS. CARTER. What's this? Oh – my guitar. Maybe they won't call for me.

MR. CARTER. *(starting off)* Are you sure you're warm enough? – Tom, do you remember coming out here with Francesca when you were six and holding a funeral over a robin redbreast?

TOM. *(lightly)* No, did I? Did I, really? – Why?

MRS. CARTER. We were just wondering, Tom.

(Exit MR. CARTER. TOM gets down on his knees preparatory to lying down again.)

TOM. I helped the squad that was picking up the trash. I rolled the ice cream cans to the truck. I showed Polly Springer how to put a marshmallow on a fork. – I've done my duty. I can rest. *(silence)* Mother, make one chord on the guitar.

(She does a slow arpeggiated chord. Silence.)

One note of music out of doors is worth ten thousand in a building. *(He again turns over on his stomach, raises himself on his elbows.)* Mother, I'm going to be the doctor that you planned to be.

MRS. CARTER. Oh! – Not an astronomer? Or a physicist?

TOM. No. That's all too far away. I'm going to be a research doctor.

MRS. CARTER. *(not hurrying)* Well, you don't have to decide now.

TOM. *(decisively)* I've decided. – Last month I thought maybe I'd be one of those new physicists. I'd find something that could stop every atomic bomb...I think others'll get there before me...Besides, that's not hard enough. Any Joe will be able to find that one of these days. I want something harder...something nearer. For instance –

(Voice offstage "MRS. CAAAR-TER." Nearer "MRS. CAAAR-TER!")

MRS. CARTER. *(raising her voice)* Ye-es. Here I am.

VOICE. The bonfire's starting. They want you to come and sing.

MRS. CARTER. Is that you, Gladys? Tell them to start singing. I'll come soon.

VOICE. All-riiight.

MRS. CARTER. You were saying you wanted to do something harder.

TOM. Harder and *nearer. (beating the ground)* There's no reason people have got to grow old so fast. I guess everybody's got to grow old some day. But I'll bet you we can discover lots of things that will put it off. I'll bet you that three hundred years from now people will think that we were just stupid about, well, about growing old so soon...I haven't any crazy idea about people living forever; but...it's funny: I don't mind getting old, but I don't like it to happen to other people. Anyway, that's decided. *(He puts his head in his arms and closes his eyes as though going to sleep.)* It's great to have something decided. *(pause)* Mother, what was the name of that nurse I had when I was real young, the southern one?

MRS. CARTER. Miss...Miss Forbes.

TOM. What was her first name?

MRS. CARTER. Let me think a minute...Maude? No. *(trouvé)* Madeleine!

TOM. Do you remember any teacher I had back then that was named...Violet?

MRS. CARTER. ...N-n-n-o.

TOM. *(dreamily)* There must have been somebody...I remember...it was like floating...and the smell of violets. Golly, I go crazy when I smell them. I'll tell you why I was so polite to old Mrs. Morris – you remember? She had perfume of violets on her. Why don't you ever wear that, Mother? Don't you like it?

MRS. CARTER. *(caught)* Why, it...never occurred to me.

TOM. That's an idea for a Christmas present, maybe.

(Voices "MRS. CAAAR-TER!")

MRS. CARTER. Here they come.

(Enter **MR. CARTER.** *)*

MR. CARTER. Do you feel like singing or not? They're making a fuss about you down there.

MRS. CARTER. Why not?

(Enter **FRANCESCA**, *running.)*

FRANCESCA. Mother, they're stamping their feet and –

MRS. CARTER. I'm coming. – I... *(She starts tuning the guitar. Going out.)* What'll I do, Tom? I'll do...

(They are out. Silence.)

FRANCESCA. The fireflies...the moon.

*(***MR. CARTER** *takes the blanket from the rock, carries it across the stage and wraps it around the rock he formerly sat on; then, sitting on the floor, leans his back against it.)*

FRANCESCA. *(cont.)* Your pipe smells so wonderful in the open air. *(she starts quietly laughing)* Papa, I'll tell you a secret. *Years* ago – when I went away to summer camp – do you know what I did? I went into your study, and I stole some of that tobacco. I put it in an envelope. And in the tent after lights out, I'd take it out and smell it...Why do they call it "Bonny Prince Charlie"? *(pause; dreamily)* I like the name of Charlie...I've never known a stupid boy named Charles. Isn't that funny? They all have something about them that's interesting. *(She starts laughing again.)* But I'll tell you something else: all Freds are terrible. Really terrible. You're the only Fred *(laughing and scarcely audible)* that I can *stand.*

MR. CARTER. Look at the moonlight just hitting the top of the boat club.

(She turns on her knees and draws in her breath, rapt.
MR. CARTER *drawing his fingers over the ground.)*

When I was a boy I found all sorts of things here. I made a collection and got a prize for it. Arrowheads and ax heads...I used to come out here and think – on this very rock.

FRANCESCA. *(glowing)* Did you? – What did you think *about?*

MR. CARTER. That someday maybe I'd have a family. That someday maybe I'd go into politics.

FRANCESCA. And now you're senator!

MR. CARTER. Tom's not interested in this place as a *human* place. He's always talking about it as a place before there were any human beings here. But even as boy, I used to think all that must have gone on here. – Initiations –

FRANCESCA. What?

MR. CARTER. Initiations into the tribe. And councils about those awful white skins. And buryings. *(pause)* On this very rock I decided to become a lawyer.

FRANCESCA. *(moving a few feet toward him on her knees)* Papa, why was I so mean to Mother?

MR. CARTER. Mean?

FRANCESCA. *(bent head, slowly)* Yes, I was. When I was telling that story about the boy from Milwaukee...mistaking Mother for an old woman, like Mrs. Cavanaugh. I knew I was mean while I was doing it. *(she sobs)* And why am I mean about Tom? I *am.* I *am. (sinking lower on her heels)* I'm terrible. I'm unforgivable. – But *why?*

MR. CARTER. Are you mean about yourself? *(She stares at him.)* Yes, now you're being mean toward yourself! – Could you imagine building a house on this point?

FRANCESCA. No…

MR. CARTER. Because you'd have to cut down so many trees?

FRANCESCA. *(slight pause)* No…I could do it without cutting down the best trees.

MR. CARTER. Why couldn't you imagine building here?

FRANCESCA. *(lightly)* I wouldn't.

MR. CARTER. No *reason?*

FRANCESCA. *(affectionately)* Why do you keep asking me when you can *see* that I don't want to answer.

MR. CARTER. Oh, I beg your pardon.

FRANCESCA. *(in a loud whisper)* I don't like this point. I've never liked it.

MR. CARTER. *(walking back and forth, right to left)* Well, isn't that funny – people feeling so differently about things.

[*(***MR. CARTER** *holds out his hand and* **FRANCESCA** *moves closer and takes his hand. They both look into the distance, lost in their thoughts and feelings, as the lights fade.)*]

End of Play

A NOTE ON THE TEXT

The place of *The Rivers Under the Earth* in Wilder's schema of short plays is ambiguous. In its first draft it was entitled *Children*. That title was dropped in later drafts. Students of Wilder have speculated that he finally meant the play to represent middle age, since *Childhood* was the title given to one of the three "Plays for Bleecker Street," produced in 1962 at Circle in the Square in New York City.

Wilder had written in his journal[1] (1) "I planned [Rivers] to arrive at a culmination illustrating – so recurrent in me – the relations between a daughter and a father." I added the final stage direction *(in brackets)* to illustrate this idea in a concluding tableau. The author's manuscript had ended with the line:

MR. CARTER. *(Walking back and forth, right to left):* Well, isn't that funny – people feeling so differently about things.

F. J. O'Neil
April 1997

---

1. *The Journals of Thornton Wilder 1939-1961*, entry 749, page 265, selected and edited by Donald Gallup, Yale University Press, 1985.

Also by
Thornton Wilder...

The Alcestiad, or A Life in the Sun

The Beaux' Stratagem (with Ken Ludwig)

The Matchmaker

Our Town

The Skin of Our Teeth

<u>Thornton Wilder One Act Series: The Seven Deadly Sins</u>

The Drunken Sisters

Bernice

The Wreck on the 5:25

A Ringing of Doorbells

In Shakespeare and the Bible

Someone From Assisi

Cement Hands

<u>Thornton Wilder One Act Series: Wilder's Classic One Acts</u>

The Long Christmas Dinner

Queens of France

Pullman Car Hiawatha

Love and How to Cure It

Such Things Only Happen in Books

The Happy Journey to Trenton and Camden

OTHER TITLES AVAILABLE FROM SAMUEL FRENCH

THE ALCESTIAD, OR A LIFE IN THE SUN

Thornton Wilder

Drama / 18m, 4f, 1 boy, extras / Exterior

Wilder retells the legend of Alcestis, who gave her life for her husband Admetus, beloved of Apollo, and was brought back from hell by Hercules. Wilder's Alcestis is a seeker after understanding, to whom "there is only one misery, and that is ignorance." Her life as wife, mother, Queen is apparently tragic: idyllic happiness is destroyed by death.

OTHER TITLES AVAILABLE FROM SAMUEL FRENCH

THE SKIN OF OUR TEETH

Thornton Wilder

*Comedy / 4 or 5m, 4 or 5f, plus many small parts w/doubling /
Interior, Exterior*

Winner of the 1943 Pulitzer Prize for Drama

This groundbreaking satiric fantasy follows the extraordinary Antrobus family down through the ages from the time of "The War," surviving flood, fire, pestilence, locusts, the ice age, the pox and the double feature, a dozen subsequent wars and as many depressions. Ultimately, they are the stuff of which heroes and buffoons are made. Their survival is a vividly theatrical testament of faith in humanity.

"Wonderfully wise...A tremendously exciting and
profound stage fable."
– Herald Tribune

OTHER TITLES AVAILABLE FROM SAMUEL FRENCH

OUR TOWN

Thornton Wilder

Drama / 17m, 7f, extras / Bare Stage

Winner of the 1938 Pulitzer Prize for Drama

In an important publishing event, Samuel French, in cooperation with the Thornton Wilder estate is pleased to release the playwright's definitive version of *Our Town*. This edition of the play differs only slightly from previous acting editions, yet it presents *Our Town* as Thornton Wilder wished it to be performed. Described by Edward Albee as "…the greatest American play ever written," the story follows the small town of Grover's Corners through three acts: "Daily Life," "Love and Marriage," and "Death and Eternity." Narrated by a stage manager and performed with minimal props and sets, audiences follow the Webb and Gibbs families as their children fall in love, marry, and eventually—in one of the most famous scenes in American theatre—die. Thornton Wilder's final word on how he wanted his play performed is an invaluable addition to the American stage and to the libraries of theatre lovers internationally.

"While all of Wilder's work is intelligent, non-synthetic and often moving, as well as funny, it is *Our Town* that makes the difference. It is probably the finest play ever written by an American."
– *Edward Albee*

"Thornton Wilder's masterpiece...An immortal tale of small town morality [and]...a classic of soft spoken theater."
– *The New York Times*

"Beautiful and remarkable one of the sagest, warmest and most deeply human scripts to have come out of our theatre...
A spiritual experience."
– *The New York Post*

SAMUELFRENCH.COM

CPSIA information can be obtained
at www.ICGtesting.com
Printed in the USA
BVHW09s1251240718
522489BV00011B/242/P